Making Writing Instruction Work

Making Writing Instruction Work

Brenda Augusta

connect2learning Courtenay, BC, Canada

© 2015 Text: Brenda Augusta
© 2015 Design: Building Connections Publishing, Inc.
© 2015 Foreword: Sandra Herbst

All rights reserved. Except as noted, no part of this publication may be reproduced or transmitted in any form or by any means — graphic, electronic, or mechanical — without prior permission of the publisher.

Printed and bound in Canada by Hignell Printing Limited.

21 20 19   6 5 4

Library and Archives Canada Cataloguing in Publication

Augusta, Brenda, author
    Making writing instruction work / Brenda Augusta.

Includes bibliographical references.
ISBN 978-1-928092-02-5 (paperback)

    1. Written communication — Study and teaching (Elementary). 2. English language — Composition and exercises — Study and teaching (Elementary). 3. Composition (Language arts) — Study and teaching (Elementary). 4. Literacy–Study and teaching (Elementary). I. Title.

LB1576.A97 2015   372.62'3044   C2015-905137-1

Project Management: Judith Hall-Patch
Editors: Sandra Herbst, Sheree North
Design: Anne Davies, Kelly Giordano, Cori Jones

Additional copies of this book are available from:

CONNECT 2 LEARNING
connect2learning
2449D Rosewall Crescent
Courtenay, BC V9N 8R9 Canada
1-800-603-9888 (toll free in North America)
1-250-703-2920
Fax: 1-250-703-2921
E-mail: books@connect2learning.com

Contents

Foreword 7
Preface 13
1. Identifying the Learning Destination 15
2. Collecting Evidence 25
3. Describing Quality 49
4. Giving Feedback 59
5. Involving Students in Self- and Peer Assessment 69
6. Planning for Success 75
Conclusion 79
Appendix A 83
Appendix B 101
Bibliography 107

Book Dedication:

*For Kevin, Scott, and Dan
You make my life work.*

Foreword

"We must know in our hearts that when we create communities wherever we are with youth that respect and care for them as individuals and invite their participation — their critical inquiry, dialogue, reflection, and action — we are creating the conditions that allow their innate potential for social competence, problem-solving, sense of identity and efficacy, and hope for the future to unfold."

Bonnie Benard

In this book, Brenda Augusta brings us into the heart and mind of a dedicated teacher inquiring into her practice. She poses tough questions and responds to them with her feet firmly planted in the classroom. Questions such as, "What is the most effective way to support writing development? What is the student's role? What is the teacher's role? How can teachers use the assessment information they gather to fine tune their teaching? How can the evidence of learning be both reliable and valid?" guide Brenda's inquiry into powerful teaching practices in the area of writing.

Researchers have "stood" beside Brenda and other teachers like her for many years, observing students learning and teachers teaching while building theories that guide more research, which in turn informs teaching. It is a wonderfully symbiotic relationship — students teach teachers, students and teachers teach researchers, researchers build theory and teach. Researchers seeking to understand classroom assessment examine teachers' practices.

When I led the Primary Program writing team in 1989, members deliberately read research in such areas as literacy and mathematics, as well as assessment. (See, for example, Stiggins and Bridgeford, 1985; Crooks, 1988; Natriello, 1987). Teachers on the writing team, selected for their contributions to both student learning and collegial learning, examined the research in light of informed teaching practices. It was an exciting time. I remember the celebration when the team linked the social sciences research methods described by Lincoln and Guba (1984) to the work of classroom teachers. If I could summarize our hours and hours of deliberation with one statement, it would be, "Every teacher is researching the learning of every child, and everything a child says, does, or creates is potentially evidence of learning." This one statement led to the revamping of our thinking about classroom assessment and what makes reliable and valid evidence of learning. These ideas became the foundation for subsequent curriculum and instruction initiatives. Over time, this insight led to the powerful work we now refer to as *assessment in the service of learning*.

Fast-forward to the present. It is evident that the world of education, teaching, learning, and assessment has changed in so many ways. Research has continued to inform teaching, assessment, and learning. There are four research-based areas[1] related to classroom assessment that serve to provide the foundation for the effective teaching of writing that Brenda Augusta describes so ably in this text.

1. The Impact on Student Learning of Classroom Assessment

Multiple studies over time clearly show that classroom assessment has the greatest impact on student learning and achievement of any educational innovation ever documented. These findings have continued to be extended across different learning contexts and supported through international research. There is increasing evidence to suggest that the learner's involvement in the assessment process is a powerful way to support self- and co-regulation. In fact, direct examination of the impact of using the strategies of Assessment for Learning – formative assessment plus the deep involvement of students in the assessment process – in classrooms has resulted in a greater understanding of how to support the learning of students who struggle, as well as those who typically do well in school.

---

1 For ease of reading, research citations are limited; however, recommended readings are listed in the Selected Bibliography.

2. Increasing Engagement and Learning Using Classroom Assessment

Researchers have shown that when teachers use Assessment for Learning to deliberately engage students in the process of learning, students learn more and teaching becomes more effective. Teaching students to engage in the formative assessment cycle themselves — what do I need to learn, what do I know now, how can I close the gap — and helping them learn to give themselves specific, descriptive feedback results in purposeful involvement, as well as greater learning and achievement gains. Over time, this process helps students develop the language of assessment so they can self-monitor, self-assess, and engage in peer assessment. As students continue to be a part of social moderation during classroom assessment and the instructional cycle, they learn to articulate what they've learned and share proof of learning with others — for example, through parent-student-teacher conferences.

3. Reliable and Valid Evidence of Student Learning

The collection of student evidence of learning from multiple sources, including products, conversations, and observations — a process called *triangulation* — does not only prepare teachers to design instruction minute-by-minute. It also provides the evidence of student learning needed to support summative judgments about student learning in relation to curriculum expectations/outcomes/standards for reporting purposes. Maxwell and Cumming (2011) state, "Concerning reliability, continuous assessment would lead to more stable judgements of student achievement (through collection of more extensive information over time and consultative judgements among teachers)" (p. 206).

4. Developing Informed Professional Judgment

Teachers develop informed professional judgment by being involved in both formal and informal processes of moderation with the purpose of coming to agreement about the quality of student evidence. Their resulting professional judgment is more reliable and valid than external tests and measures. Being involved in a process of social moderation has been shown to result in adults "learning to produce valid and reliable judgements that are consistent with one another and with stated achievement standards" (Adie, Klenowski, and Wyatt-Smith, 2012). It is also part of what caused the Assessment Reform Group in a publication titled, *The role of teachers in the assessment of learning* (2006), to say that teachers' professional judgment is more reliable and valid than external tests when they are engaged in looking at student work, co-constructing criteria, creating a scoring guide, scoring the work, and checking for inter-rater reliability. Teachers, even with students as young as five and six years of age, are experiencing the same kinds of results with a classroom version of social moderation.

As you embark on reading *Making Writing Instruction Work*, consider what really matters — students and their learning. It is through experiences such as those that result from the work Brenda describes that we build relationships with children and invite them to engage in the kind of critical inquiry, dialogue, reflection, and action that make a better future for all of us more possible. You make a difference in the lives of children every day. I know the ideas in this book can help you make a positive difference — right now.

Anne Davies, Ph.D.

Recommended Readings (Selected)

The Impact on Student Learning of Classroom Assessment

Black, P. and D. Wiliam. 1998. Assessment and classroom learning. *Assessment in Education* 5, no. 1: 7-75.

Harlen, W. and R. Deakin Crick. 2003. Testing and motivation for learning. *Assessment in Education* 10, no. 2: 169-208.

Hattie, J. and H. Timperley. 2007. The power of feedback. *Review of Educational Research* 77, no. 1: 81-112.

Increasing Engagement and Learning Using Classroom Assessment

Andrade, H. 2011. Foreword. In K. Gregory, C. Cameron, and A. Davies, *Self-Assessment and Goal Setting*, 2nd Edition, pp. 7-16. Courtenay, BC: Connections Publishing.

Chappuis, J., Stiggins, R., Chappuis, S., and J. Arter. 2012. *Classroom Assessment for Student Learning: Doing It Right — Using It Well*, 2nd Edition. Upper Saddle River, NJ: Pearson Education.

Wiliam, D. 2007. Keeping learning on track: classroom assessment and the regulation of learning. In F. K. Lester Jr. (Ed.), *Second Handbook of Mathematics Teaching and Learning* (pp. 1053-1098). Greenwich, CT: Information Age Publishing.

Reliable and Valid Evidence of Student Learning

Davies, A. 2000. *Making Classroom Assessment Work*, 1st Edition. Courtenay, BC: Connections Publishing.

Davies, A. 2011. *Making Classroom Assessment Work*, 3rd Edition. Courtenay, BC: Connections Publishing.

Manitoba Education, Citizenship and Youth. 2006. *Rethinking Classroom Assessment with Purpose in Mind*. Winnipeg, MB: Government of Manitoba.

Ministry of Education, Ontario. 2010. *Growing Success*. Toronto, ON: Government of Ontario.

Developing Informed Professional Judgment

Assessment Reform Group (ARG). 2006. *The role of teachers in the assessment of learning*. Pamphlet produced by Assessment Systems for the Future project (ASF). http://arrts.gtcni.org.uk/gtcni/handle/2428/4617.

Adie, L., Klenowski, V., and Wyatt-Smith, C. 2012. Towards an understanding of teacher judgement in the context of social moderation. *Educational Review*, 64 (2), 223-240.

Herbst, S. and Davies, A. 2014. *A Fresh Look at Grading and Reporting in High Schools*. Courtenay, BC: Connections Publishing and Bloomington, IN: Solution Tree Press.

Preface

I remember learning to read. I remember being so thrilled with myself that I read out loud, for the pure joy of it, for hours on end. I remember asking my mom, a Grade 2 teacher and therefore incapable of turning me away, "Can I have paper? I need to write. How do you spell Mississippi?" I was six and had not yet heard about writing about what you know. My Christmas and birthday gifts always included books and writing materials, anything to do with words. I had it all: diaries, journals, autograph books, over-size notebooks, teeny tiny notebooks, and paper of all sizes and colours.

This love for the printed word has never gone away. Through all of the years of juggling family life, work life, life, I have eked out time to read and write. Friends and colleagues (my family is used to it) have always asked me, "How do you find time to read?" and "How can you read so much when you have a young family?" and "Aren't you too tired to read after teaching all day?" My response has always been, and continues to be, that I am prepared to give up sleep to make time for reading and writing. I don't tell you this as a prescription for a good night's sleep or as a means to a well-rested body and mind. I tell you this in order to demonstrate the value I place upon reading and writing in my own life.

This love for the printed word is largely responsible for my life's work. I believed in the power of reading and writing so much that I was compelled to share it. And here is where the plot gets interesting. The reading side of the literacy equation has always made sense to me, right from my very first course as an undergraduate. The theory and the views expressed by the experts all worked when I brought them into my classroom instruction. My students not only learned to read; they learned to value reading and to see it as part of a life well lived.

Not so with writing.

For more than two decades, the theories and experts all seemed contradictory to me. They did not come together in my mind, or my practice, in a cohesive, clear way. I would think that I had one piece figured out and then questions would arise in another part. I could never see the whole. And because I could not, neither could my students.

This book is a description of writing as I now see it. It is a synthesis of the big ideas of assessment in the service of learning — as described by Dylan Wiliam, Paul Black, Anne Davies, and Rick Stiggins, among others — and the work of writing teachers such as Donald Graves, Regie Routman, Lucy Calkins, Penny Kittle, and others. It is a framework built on the principles of assessment that makes sense in relation to the teaching of writing — beginning with the curriculum, moving into decision-making about instruction (assessment for and of learning) and communicating with parents and students about each student's progress as a writer.

Chapter 1 explores the identification of a clear and specific learning destination, both for us as teachers and for our students. Chapter 2 focuses on the types of evidence that we, both teachers and students, could collect as we monitor progress toward the identified learning destination. Chapter 3 discusses the various ways that quality can be described for the learners. In Chapter 4, the role of feedback is highlighted, and Chapter 5 describes ways that students can be engaged in self- and peer assessment. Chapter 6 pulls it all together, showing how a four-step assessment plan (Davies, 2000, 2011) allows us to plan for six to eight weeks of writing instruction.

School is a busy place and teachers are busy people. But even at my busiest, I have time for a four-step plan that is based in research and validated practice and allows me to make sense of something as important as the teaching of writing. I hope that you do too.

Chapter 1
Identifying the Learning Destination

Where are we going?

Why are we writing?

Who are we writing for?

Rick Stiggins (2004) is often credited with saying that students can reach any target that they know about and that stands still for them. Depending upon where I was in my journey as a writing teacher, my students may have thought the target was:

- Changing a few words in a frame sentence.
- Writing "five star" sentences.
- Writing a journal entry each day beginning with "I got up" and ending with "I went to bed. The End."
- Doing their best spelling.
- Writing to make their teacher happy.
- Writing longer pieces each year.
- Drafting, revising, editing, publishing. Repeat.

In my head, the target was much more specific and clear. My goal for each and every student was that they **Get Better At Writing** (bold font and capitals are intentional to illustrate the irony of this statement and its inability to inform my teaching). The teaching of writing remained a huge, somewhat mysterious task until I realized that I really didn't know my curriculum well enough. I didn't know exactly what I wanted my students to know, understand, do, and be able to articulate. Yet reading the curriculum, in fact poring over it, was not enough. I needed to take it apart and put it back together in a way that made sense to me and served the needs of the writers whom I was teaching.

Deconstructing the Curriculum

I can conceive of only two surefire ways of taking the curriculum apart and restructuring it so that I know it, own it, and can teach from it. In these two different but related processes, it is possible to bring clarity to ourselves and to our students regarding where we are going and ensuring that we have done all that the curriculum calls upon us to do. In the first example, we sort and categorize the details.

Beginning with the Details

- Considering both the front matter of the curriculum and the specific learning outcomes, copy all that pertain to writing. This can be done electronically, cutting and pasting what you need from the curriculum into a Word document.

- Print this as a list with one statement per line. Cut out each statement as a strip.

- Sort and group the strips in a way that makes sense to your team. (I hope you are working with a partner or a team, as this is definitely made easier and more efficient with collaboration.)

- Look at your categories. How many are there? Do any of the categories naturally fit together? What names work for each category?

- Considering the number of terms you have, the nature of your categories, the needs of your students, and where you are in the school year, you can roughly plot out the year, assigning some categories to specific terms and knowing that some will be a part of each term.

- Thinking about the next six to eight weeks, decide which categories are appropriate. This becomes the learning destination for writing in this time period.
- Ensure that the learning destination is written in student-friendly terms. For me, that means using "I can" statements or statements describing what students need to know, understand, do, and say (Tomlinson & Moon, 2013; Wiggins & McTighe, 2005).

Recently, I was working with a group of Grade 3 teachers in Manitoba. After following the process outlined above, we had three large categories that they decided could work — one per term:

- Personal Writing
- Writing to Respond
- Writing Informational Text

We also had several categories that we thought would be ongoing throughout the year:

- Self-assessment and goal setting
- Conventions/rules of writing
- Working as a community of writers

To refine our learning destination to the point where we could teach from it and our students could understand it, we elected to work on "Writing to Respond" for the next six to eight weeks. We also decided that we would focus on two genres: letters and reviews. Based on these decisions, we wrote the following learning destination:

Students will:

Know:
Various genres and forms have distinguishing features. Letters and reviews have some features in common and some that are form specific.

Understand:
Studying samples of letters and reviews helps us co-construct criteria for writing in these genres. Understanding and applying the criteria help us produce quality writing.

Do:
Use the descriptions of quality (models, shared writes, criteria, feedback) to write letters and reviews.

Say:
Describe the features of letters and reviews and how good writers use them as they write for a reader.

We were also able to identify the big ideas we would be working on all year.

Students will:

Know:
Their strengths and next steps as writers.

Understand:
Writers continually self-assess and improve their writing, making it better for their reader.

Do:
Work with various small and large groups to support each other as writers.

Say:
Describe evidence that they have met criteria for letters and reviews. (See pages 34-35 for pictures of this process.)

Beginning with the Big Ideas

In the second approach, we think about the big ideas of what we want to teach in writing, the "why" behind the specific learning outcomes. These big ideas are found in many places:

> Most English Language Arts curricula contain big ideas that, with just a little tweaking, are understandable by students. Looking at some of the Manitoba Grade 1 English Language Arts outcomes, shown in Figure 1.1 on page 19, I might start with:
>
> - Writers and readers talk and write to share what they know and feel with others.

- Writers and readers use what they know about sounds, letters, words, and pictures to tell their story for their readers and to keep themselves writing.
- Writers and readers learn from each other and support each other.

Figure 1.1

Grade 1 Manitoba ELA Curriculum
Specific Learning Outcomes that could connect to writing free verse poetry:
- listen to and acknowledge experiences and feelings shared by others
- choose to read and write with and for others
- describe new experiences and ideas
- connect new experiences and information with prior knowledge
- share feelings and moods evoked by oral, literary, and media texts
- tell, draw, and write about self and family
- participate in shared listening, reading, and viewing experiences using texts from a variety of forms, genres, and cultural traditions
- experiment with parts of words, word combinations, and word patterns for a variety of purposes
- use sound-symbol relationships and visual memory to spell familiar words
- capitalize the first letters of names, the beginnings of statements, and the pronoun "I"
- use periods
- experiment with words and sentence patterns using specific structures
- work in cooperative and collaborative partnerships and groups
- take turns sharing information and ideas
- help others and ask others for help
- identify and assume roles necessary for maintenance of group process
- use a variety of forms to express and explore familiar events, ideas, and information
- recognize different forms and genres of oral, literary, and media texts
- appreciate repetition, rhyme, and rhythm in shared language experiences
- create original texts to communicate and demonstrate understanding of forms and techniques
- demonstrate interest in and suggest enhancements for own and others' work
- group and sort ideas and information to make sense
- rephrase and represent to clarify ideas
- strive for consistency in letter size and shape
- print letters legibly from left to right horizontally, using lines on a page as a guide
- check for completeness of work and add details and enhancements

- Writers can choose to write in different ways or forms depending upon their purpose and audience.
- Writers think about their writing and how to make it clear and interesting for themselves and their readers.

Writing experts also contribute to the thinking around big ideas:

- From Regie Routman (2005) in Writing Essentials, I might consider: Writers care about their readers. Writers change their minds while they write. Writers talk about their writing. Writers keep themselves writing.
- From Lucy Calkins (2010), I might borrow the idea of units of study and write big ideas such as: I can write in response to my reading. I can write to persuade my reader. I can write to teach about a topic. I can write to share my opinion.

Published continua like Bonnie Campbell Hill's developmental writing continuum (2001) can lead us to big ideas:

- Writers follow the rules of writing.
- Writers work to keep the reader's interest and attention.
- Writers use strategies and techniques to improve their writing.
- Writers self-assess and set goals.
- Writers learn from other writers.

Once we have our big ideas, we cut apart the strips from the previous process and sort them under the appropriate heading. This step clarifies and adds depth to the big idea and allows us to know with confidence that we are teaching all that we are responsible for. We know our big ideas are complete when, to use a technology-based metaphor, we can "double click" on them and see all of the curricular outcomes that apply to writing. See Appendix A for more examples.

Making Our Teaching and Learning Authentic

To this point, I have only been talking about the curriculum. The truth of the matter is that we teach writers. Teaching, like reading, is a transactional activity. Learning occurs in the interplay between each learner and the curriculum, with the teacher as mediator. Just as each reader interacts with an author's words in his or her own way, not all writers experience learning to write in exactly the same way. This is where the professional judgment of the teacher becomes so critical. Professional judgment is not something we use only at the end of the process to write report cards. It is something we use every day as we consider the ever-changing, moment-by-moment evidence right in front of us.

In order to make the professional judgments necessary to decide on the learning destination for my particular group of students at this point in time, I need some baseline data. I need writing samples to see what they already know and have under their control. I must observe them as they write, looking for evidence about their process. Do they think about the reader? Do they reread as they write? Do they use the word wall? I need to engage them in conversations about writing and writers, both with me and with each other. Conversations help me discover what they are interested in, what they know and care about, what they wonder, and what they are passionate about. When I collect this kind of triangulated evidence (Davies 2000, 2011), I can connect the curriculum with my learners. I can write "better" learning destinations when I have a specific audience in mind, as I think about the students in front of me right now.

Just as we can write more authentic learning destinations with specific students in mind, student writers also need to know for whom they are writing (Routman, 2005). The answer to this question must be part of the learning destination:

- We are writing a book for our classroom library that tells what we are really good at.
- We are writing restaurant reviews for the students of our school.
- We are writing a book about the fur trade for other Grade 5 students.

As important as who we are writing for is why we are writing. When I add an authentic purpose to the above statements, I make the learning destination more explicit and more motivating:

- We are writing a book for our classroom library that tells what we are really good at so that we get to know each other better.
- We are writing restaurant reviews for the students of our school because kids will be interested in knowing about restaurants that other kids recommend.
- We are writing a book for other Grade 5 students about the fur trade because the ones we've been reading don't make it interesting from a kid's point of view.

My learning destinations need to communicate a real purpose, both for a specific writing task and for writing in general. Why are we writing and for whom are we writing? In Figure 1.2, notice how the addition of a real audience and authentic purpose enriches the learning destination, beginning on page 17.

Figure 1.2

Initial Learning Destination	Learning Destination with Audience and Purpose
Know: Various genres and forms have distinguishing features. Letters and reviews have some features in common and some that are form specific. **Understand:** Studying samples of letters and reviews helps us co-construct criteria for writing in these genres. Understanding and applying the criteria helps us produce quality writing. **Do:** Use the descriptions of quality (models, shared writes, criteria, feedback) to write letters and reviews. **Say:** Describe the features of letters and reviews and how good writers use them as they write for a reader.	**Know:** Various genres and forms have distinguishing features (features of letters and reviews). **Understand:** Writers write for many purposes, audiences, and genres. Some details of the criteria for quality writing vary depending upon the genre/form and some are constant. **Do:** Write letters for a real audience and purpose in response to an event. Write book reviews of new books in the library for other students. **Say:** Can talk about whom they are writing for and why.

Now that the learning destination is clear to me, I can make it clear to my students, and I can differentiate the learning destination based on my baseline data and the evidence students provide on a day-to-day basis. So many other areas can now be considered. I can think about the kinds of evidence we might collect — the conversations, observations, and products that will prove to me and my students where they are in relation to the target. Knowing the learning destination and comparing it to the baseline data also make it clear to me the kinds of samples my students will need to see, the criteria we will need to co-construct, and the modelling I will need to do. I can see the mini-lessons that might follow, the genres we might study, the conferences we might have, and the conversations we might engage in. But first, I must know the curriculum and make it my own.

Chapter 2
Collecting Evidence

What does this writer know?

What can this writer do?

What is this writer's next step?

What kind of evidence might we collect before, during, and after the writing?

Many years ago, I was co-teaching in a Grade 2 writers' workshop. The teacher and I were looking at one student's writing portfolio together. It was filled with eight or ten drafts, each as challenging for us to read as the one before. Each page included many large, black dots scattered willy-nilly all over the page. As if uttering a profound truth, I said to myself, "This kid does not know how to use periods!" and wrote it down in my notebook.

Our instruction would have continued to miss the mark if we had not followed this initial look at the student's writing with an observation. Later in the workshop, I happened to catch sight of the writer in question taking a big breath and making a mark on her page, taking another big breath and making another mark. Curiosity piqued, I pulled up a chair and said, "Please tell me about what you are doing." She looked up at me and replied, "I am figuring out where the periods go, just like you said." There was a system for the placement of periods on her page? And I was responsible for it??

"Tell me more," I encouraged.

"Well, yesterday you said the periods go where you breathe. So I write it all out, and then I go back and see where I need to breathe and that is where I put the periods. Just like you said."

The writing sample alone could never have revealed this misconception. Without the benefit of the observation and resulting conversation, I could not possibly have understood the student's thinking or provided the "just-in-time" instruction that she needed.

Before Writing

To know where to begin my teaching, I need to know where my students are. To know whether something needs to be part of a whole group lesson, a small group session, or an individual conference, I need to know where my students are. Through the research on assessment (Davies, 2000, 2011; Lincoln & Guba, 1984), we know that when we triangulate — consider products, observations, and conversations — our evidence becomes reliable and valid.

Before beginning instruction on a writing topic or genre, I need to collect data that shows me in the moment what students know and can do independently. Students can later use this evidence to compare to samples that I provide and to their subsequent writing. To extend the example from Chapter 1, if we are going to write letters (or reviews, journal entries, free verse poetry...), I need to collect some evidence before we ever begin.

Products

I have students write a letter, reminding them to use all that they know about good writing in general and letter writing specifically. Because I want to know what they can do independently, I have them write without a lot of fanfare. I explain that the purpose is to show me what they already know about letter writing and what we will need to do in order to improve and, ultimately, to reach the learning destination. This sample becomes important to the students later on in the process, as they use it as a point of comparison to writing they will do after instruction.

Conversations

Simply looking at the letters does not afford enough evidence to make quality decisions about what is known and what needs to come next. Asking students to tell me about their letter in a conference is one way to bring conversation into the picture.

Tell me about your letter.

What makes it a letter?

How did you decide what to write about?

How did you make your letter interesting for the reader?

Sometimes these conversations are written. Students might be asked to make a list of what they know about writing letters in their writer's notebook, journal, or learning log. Sometimes these conversations are between students as I listen in: *Turn and talk to your partner about what you know about writing a letter.*

Sometimes these conversations are recorded or filmed using hand-held technology. In all instances, the talk about the writing helps me understand more about what each writer knows, understands, and is able to do. It enriches my understanding of where each writer is, and where he or she needs to go next.

Observations

I observe the students as they write, making general notes on a class list or anecdotal record sheet, or recording answers to a specific focus question such as:

Is the writer able to choose someone to write to and get started?

What does the writer do if he or she gets "stuck"?

What resources available in the classroom does the writer use (word walls, charts, classmates…)?

Pulling It All Together

As I consider the triangulated baseline data for each writer, I ask myself:

- What does this writer already know?
- What can this writer already do?
- What is this writer's next step?

As I consider the triangulated baseline data for the class as a whole, I ask myself:

- *What do these writers already know?*
- *What can these writers already do?*
- *What features of letters do they all need to learn about?*
- *What features of letters do some of them need to learn about?*

The answers to these questions become lists — lists of writers who are able to choose a person to write to and those who need support, lists showing those who know the physical layout of a letter and those who do not yet know, lists showing those who write with their reader in mind and how they do it. The lists become the focus of mini-lessons, some for the whole group, some for small groups, and some for individual writers.

During Writing

Once I move into the instructional sequence, I need evidence that will tell me and the students where they are in relation to the learning destination. Planning for this now, in advance of teaching, ensures that the evidence I collect aligns with the learning destination. It also allows for the ongoing, moment-by-moment assessment that tells me what to do next, whether "next" refers to the next words to come out of my mouth, the next lesson I will teach, the next conference I will have, or the next writing topic we will tackle.

Conversations

- After each model, shared write, or public conference, I ask the students to turn and talk about what they learned from the sample. Often, I chart this for the group as a means of capturing the conversation and as a support for those who may need it.
- I listen to partner and small group conversations, asking them to report back to the whole group.
- I use sticky notes or exit slips and ask students to respond to the question: *What is important in writing a letter?*

- I conduct "on the fly" conferences as students are writing, getting a snapshot of their current thinking and ability to apply the ideas I am modelling.

The next step is to analyze these conversations, asking questions such as:

- Who is contributing?
- What are they saying? What are they not saying?
- What does this tell me about what they know?
- What further descriptions of quality might be needed?

Observations

We cannot leave observations to chance, hoping that we see and record anecdotes that will help us understand what is going on with each writer. Thinking about our learning destination, I identify possible focus questions and opportunities for observation:

- What are students noticing in the samples?
- Who is participating in the shared writing? What are they contributing?
- Who is able to talk about his/her writing?
- Who is using the resources in the room?
- Who is able to get started independently? Who needs support?
- Who is able to keep himself/herself writing?
- What further descriptions of quality might be needed?

I can add to this list as we move further into the project or unit of study, but I find it most helpful to begin thinking about it when I am doing my big picture planning. At this stage — before I am already in the middle of it — I am able to ensure that my learning destination makes sense and will be clear to all, that the evidence we collect will be connected to our learning destination, and that my teaching includes the samples of quality these students need in order to arrive at the learning destination. It is not set in stone; I change it and add to it all the time — when the evidence in front of me informs me that I should.

Products

I include partial products in this category as well, because there is much to be learned as writers are in process. Each draft has the potential to teach me something about a writer. There is no need to wait until the piece is published, the point at which most young writers believe they are done. Rather, partial products allow me to look closely at student writing and artifacts related to writing and ask myself more questions:

- Review stickies and exit slips. What are they noticing? What are they not noticing that I want them to? How can I model more of that?

- Read drafts looking for specifics of the learning destination or the criteria. Talk about what you are seeing and not seeing with the class. If revision is one of the criteria and you are not seeing it, model it in the next lesson, telling students that you are coming back to it because only ten out of twenty students are doing it. All need to be on board because this is something good writers do.

After Writing

At the end of the unit of study, it is time to look again at all three areas to know what students have learned as writers. Some of this evidence will be looked at in ways that tell the student and me what he or she knows about writing in a specific genre. Some of it will be considered in light of what the student knows about writing in general.

Conversations

- Conference with all students individually, asking them to show where and how they have met the criteria for a quality letter in their final draft.

- Ask students to tell or write about what makes a good letter.

- Ask students to describe the audience and purpose for the letter written.

- Consider exit slips and stickies.

Observations
- Does the writer use the criteria as a resource?
- Is the writer able to identify evidence of the criteria in models, shared writes, his or her own writing?
- Complete teacher checklists.

Products
- One letter brought to publication
- One letter marked up to show evidence of criteria
- Two to four letters in draft form

The better and richer the evidence collected, the better decisions we are able to make as teachers (Stiggins, 2014). Professional judgment is made up of the multitude of decisions we make daily about what sense students are making of the experiences they are having in writing workshop and whether or not they can apply them to their own writing. Our job is to keep teaching until they can.

The following pages of photographs are courtesy of students and teachers who have opened their classrooms and their learning to me.

Describing the Learning Destination

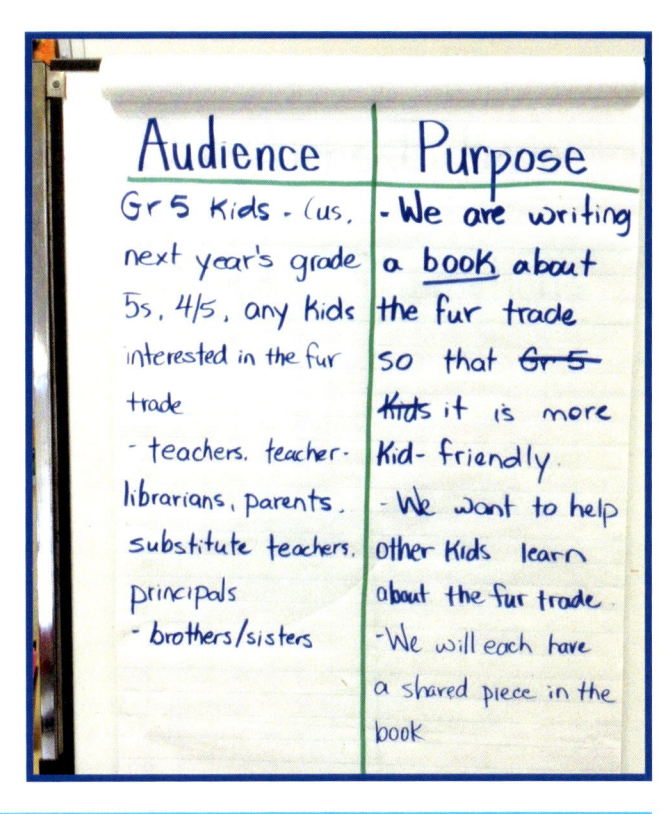

Audience	Purpose
Gr 5 kids - (us, next year's grade 5s, 4/5, any kids interested in the fur trade - teachers, teacher-librarians, parents, substitute teachers, principals - brothers/sisters	- We are writing a **book** about the fur trade so that ~~Gr 5 kids~~ it is more kid-friendly. - We want to help other kids learn about the fur trade. - We will each have a shared piece in the book

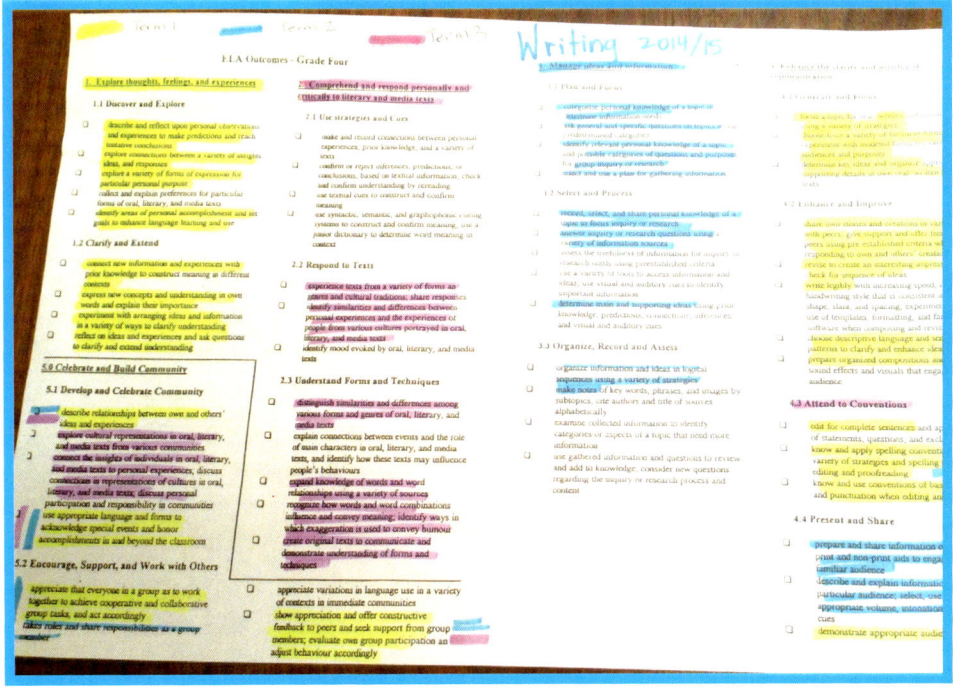

Making Writing Instruction Work

Describing the Learning Destination

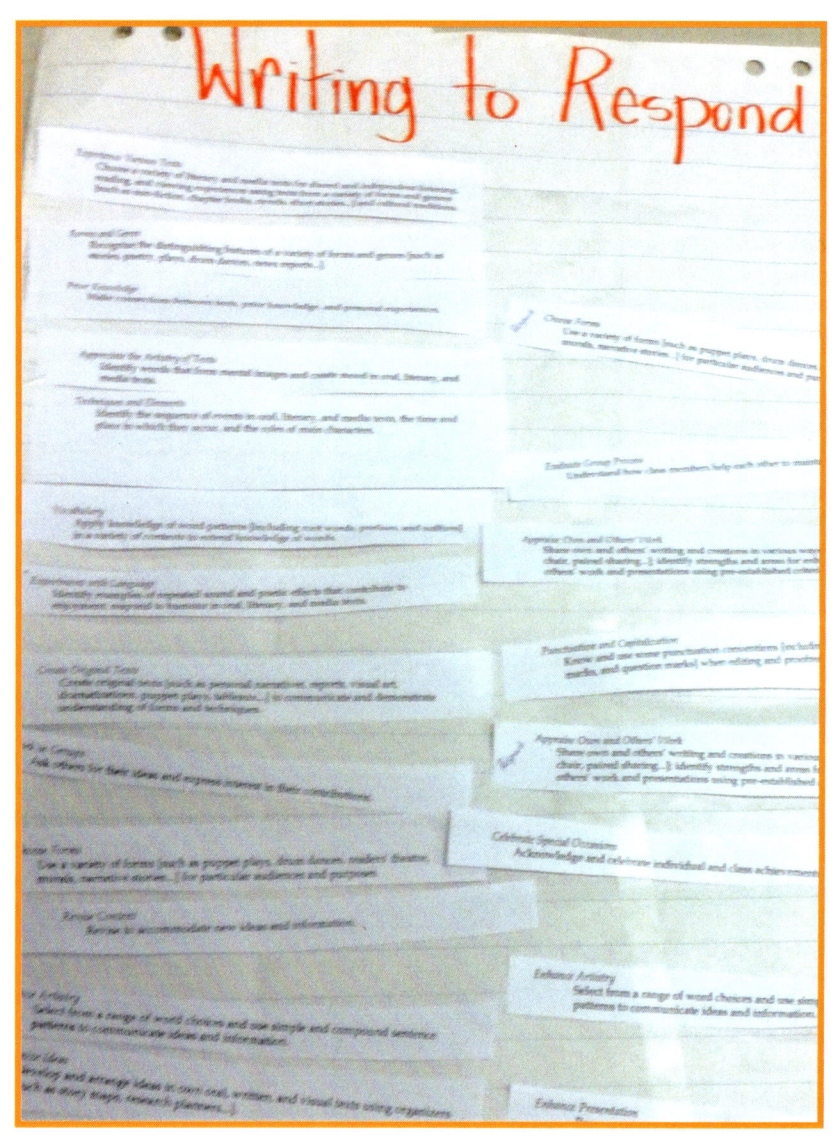

Writing to Respond

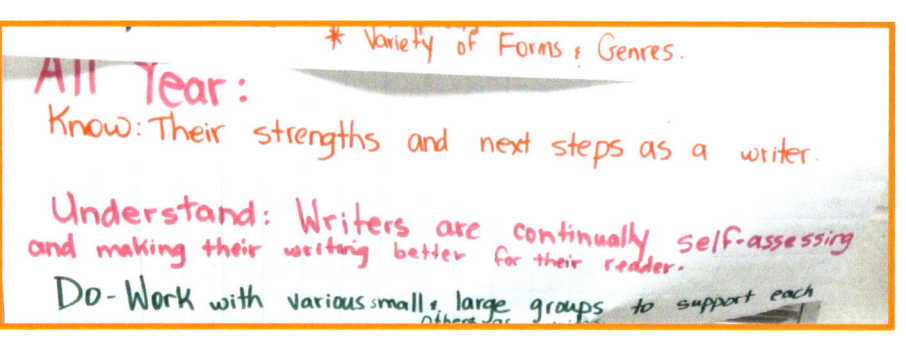

---

*Variety of Forms & Genres.

All Year:

Know: Their strengths and next steps as a writer.

Understand: Writers are continually self-assessing and making their writing better for their reader.

Do - Work with various small & large groups to support each

Describing the Learning Destination

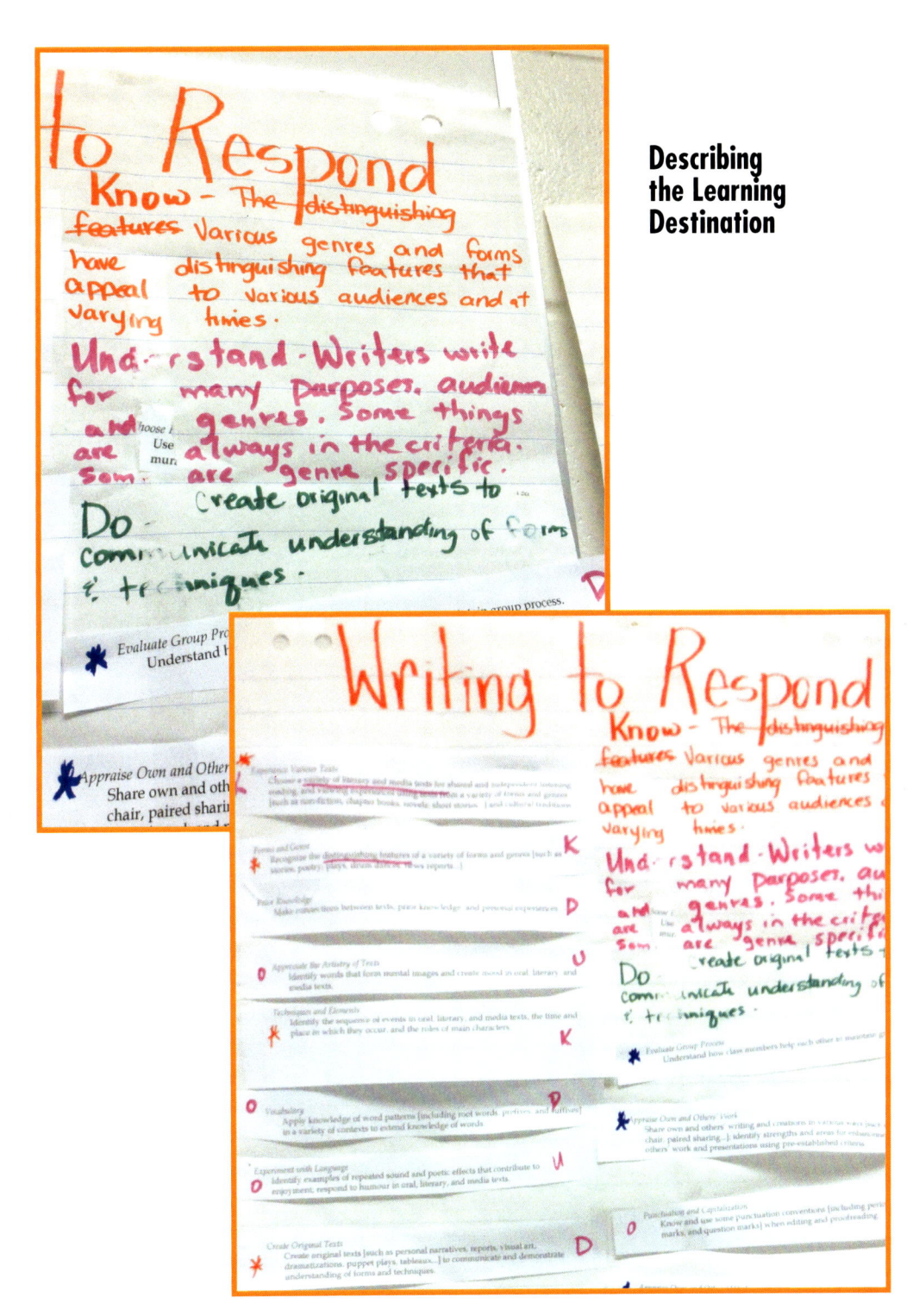

Teacher Modelling

Amelia Earhart   JAN 13 / JAN 15 / JAN 16th

Amelia the air 'rebbel, began her journey ~~in~~ July 24, 1897 in ~~Kas~~ Atchison Kansas. Here she was ~~born~~ born into a family that didn't follow gender rules. She belived that woman have as much courage as men. They let Amelia do things that girls didn't typic[ally]... Then at the age of ~~23~~ Dec 27 8 m she got a ride in a plane and in love with ~~pra~~ ~~flight~~...

She ~~Amelia~~ quickly became famous ~~becs~~ as she started to break records. ~~She~~ In 1932 ~~As~~ she was the first to cross the Atlantic Ocean in a plane called Friendship and ~~her journey only took 20 hrs.~~ ~~in 1932.~~ Her next amazing feat was to try and ~~cros~~ fly around the world in a Lockheed Model 10 Electra. Sadly ~~she~~ her plane went missing and was never found. When WWI broke out Amelia decided to be~~come~~ a nurse in Canada. To this day she is still a ~~role model~~ inspiration for people all around the world, especially young fliers.

With thanks to Leigh Stachniak Whalen, Winnipeg, MB

Teacher Modelling

Oct. 24

I have always been a "book whisperer." I take ∧ pride in finding ~~just~~ the right book for every occaision. It started when I was a kid and the oldest of 8 cousins. It was my job to ~~p~~ select their Chr... When I was a t... I chose books f...

^immense

the children I babysat. I loved when somebody would say, "Brenda, this is perfect for me!!" or "Has this author written anything else?"

Today I recommend books to teachers,— books to read to their students, ~~for~~ books for Science, books for professional learning, ... books for the sheer joy of reading.

Teacher Modelling

Dear Daniel,

Some people think that heroes must be folks who ~~that~~ have lived long on this earth. Not me. I know that age has nothing to do with it. My hero is a twenty-four year old, wise-cracking, ——— Kid. This may be sounding familiar to you ... and if should. YOU are my hero.

Why? You ~~are~~ never, ever give up. In ~~the face~~ the darkest of times, you always rise above it all and help the see the humour.

When people ask how I can handle your cancer diagnosis, I say

Your courage, your belief in yourself and your unfailingly positive attitude leave me in awe. On top of all of this, you are hysterically funny. Only you can ~~\~~ help me see anything ~~funny~~ amusing about ~~a~~ thirteen volumes of hospital chart or cancer at 22. You are my inspiration. I am more courageous, more alive because of you.

Teacher Modelling

Dec. 17, 2014

Dear Santa,

~~I~~ would like ^!
~~The~~ North Pole.
~~Santa's~~ Your workshop could use my organizational skills. I have managed a classroom with twenty or more children
^That's 600 ✗ kids!!
for thirty years. I have listened ^to and solved problems for many, ~~many~~ MANY children. I think working with elves ^would be a lot like working with ~~is~~ children.

I am experienced at time management a Grade 1 teacher who could tell time. My other duties as MOM ~~to~~ of two sons ~~has~~ have prepared me as well. I have made a To Do list for them every week. ~~I~~ The Head Elf needs to be able to delegate ~~to~~ so that all the jobs can get done.

Santa, I would love to work at the North Pole. I have lived in ~~Win~~ Winterpeg all of my life ... so I know snow. Please hir me as your Head Elf. You won't regret it.

Sincerely,
Brenda August

Making Writing Instruction Work

Teacher Modelling

Hoover le blanc

Il était une fois un chien qui n'aimait pas sa couleur. Il était tout blanc. Son nom était Hoover.

Lundi, Hoover a trouvé (trouva) un champ de fraises. Il se roula dans les fraises et devient tout rouge. « Cela ne va pas du tout. Je ressemble à une tomate! », s'exclama Hoover. Alors il retourna à la maison et se lava.

« Mauvaise idée. Je pue! », dit Hoover.

Alors Hoover retourna à la maison et se lava. Il s'exclama : « Je suis très beau tout blanc. Je ne veux plus changer de couleur. »

Après ce jour, Hoover resta tout blanc. Il n'alla plus dans l'enclos de cochons!

With thanks to École Howden, Winnipeg, MB

Shared Writing

Amazing Art with Alice

These are some of our paintings of the Seven Teachings. We drew animals from the Seven Teachings that represent us the most. Our paintings show Norval Morrisseau's art style. We all had so much fun painting our animals we drew with our guest artist, Mrs Kulyk. Our class used water colour paper, acrylic paints, and black Sharpie markers to make our paintings. Hope you all like our artwork!

By Grade 2 Students from Mrs Sherby and Pani Nazarevich's class

With thanks to Springfield Heights School, Winnipeg, MB

~~We Are~~ Friendship Expert

We are PERFECT at making friends! We are respectful to everyone. We play fair. We help each other. If someone is hurt we help them. We say "Hi" to someone new, to introduce our... When someone is stuck on a word in a book, we help them figure it out. We include everyone. and make them happy all day long.

Making Writing Instruction Work 41

Shared Writing

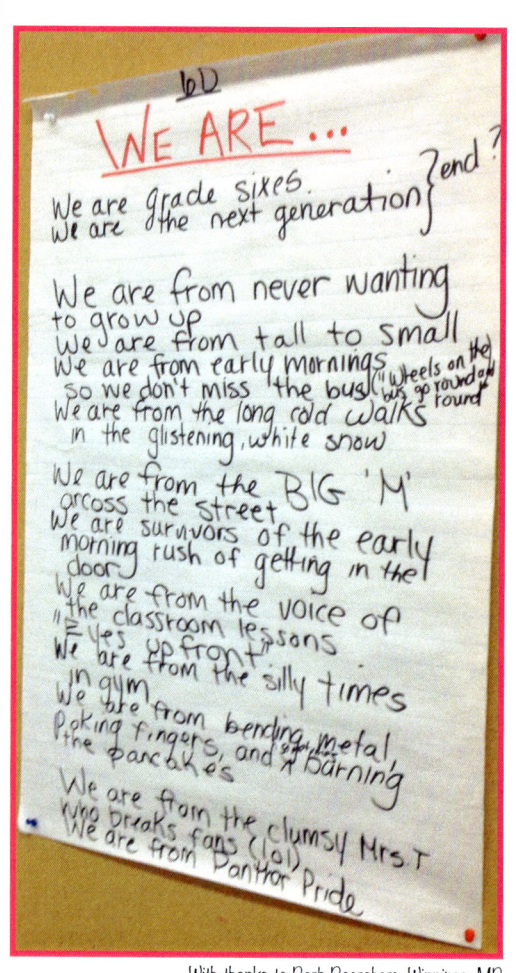

What Good Problem-Solvers Do:

1.) Read the problem from beginning to end.
2.) What is the problem telling me? (what do I already know)
3.) What do I need to find out?
4.) Are there any special conditions?

With thanks to Springfield Heights School, Winnipeg, MB

WE ARE...

We are grade sixes.
We are the next generation? end?

We are from never wanting to grow up
We are from tall to small
We are from early mornings "wheels on the
so we don't miss the bus" wheels go round and round
We are from the long cold walks
in the glistening, white snow

We are from the BIG 'M'
across the street
We are survivors of the early
morning rush of getting in the door
We are from the voice of
the classroom lessons
"≡ Yes, up front"
We are from the silly times
in gym
We are from bending metal,
poking fingers, and burning
the pancakes

We are from the clumsy Mrs T
who breaks fans (lol)
We are from Panther Pride

With thanks to Barb Boerchers, Winnipeg, MB

Unfortunately, it was a downpour outside today!
It was like it was raining cats and dogs.
I saw dark, black clouds in the sky. All of my friends and I couldn't go out for any recesses. We were stuck inside for the whole day. We were starting to feel go stir crazy.
Fortunately, I LOVE the rain! It is fun to catch small little droplets of rain on my pink slimy tongue. Lucky for me, I have tall polka dotted boots, an umbrella, and a raincoat so I can dance in the rain, bike in the rain, and splash in the puddles

With thanks to Rivers Elementary School, Rivers, MB

Shared Writing

"L'art et les pourquois par les amis de la salle 1b

Ce mois, nous avons eu beaucoup d'artiste dans l'école. Ils ont partagé des contes pourquoi avec nous.

Ensuite, nous avons écrit nos propre contes. C'est une histoire d'un animal canadien et comment il est devenu comme il est aujourd'hui.

finalement, Mme A. Kulyk est venu nous presenter l'artiste Noval Morrisseau. Nous avons fait une peinture acrylique de notre animal canadien. Voici notre travail.

With thanks to Springfield Heights School, Winnipeg, MB

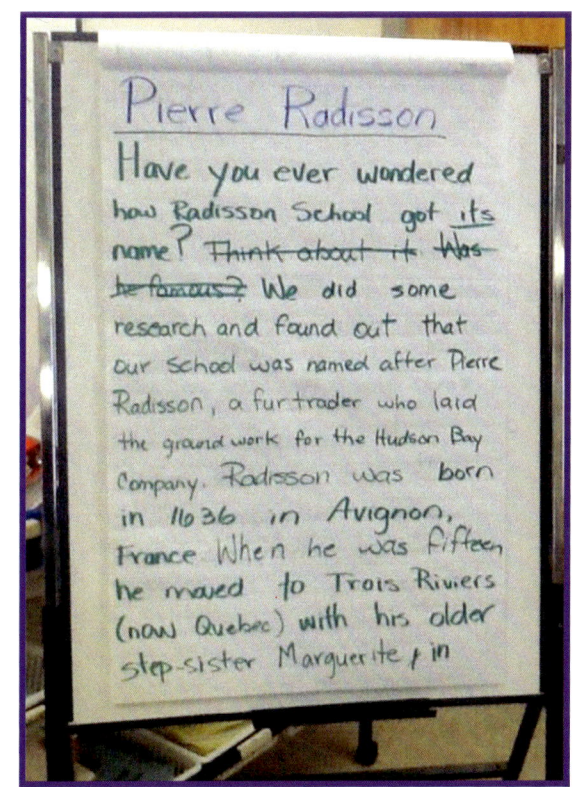

Pierre Radisson

Have you ever wondered how Radisson School got its name? ~~Think about it Was be famous?~~ We did some research and found out that our school was named after Pierre Radisson, a fur trader who laid the groundwork for the Hudson Bay Company. Radisson was born in 1636 in Avignon, France. When he was fifteen he moved to Trois Riviers (now Quebec) with his older step-sister Marguerite, in

Co-constructing Criteria

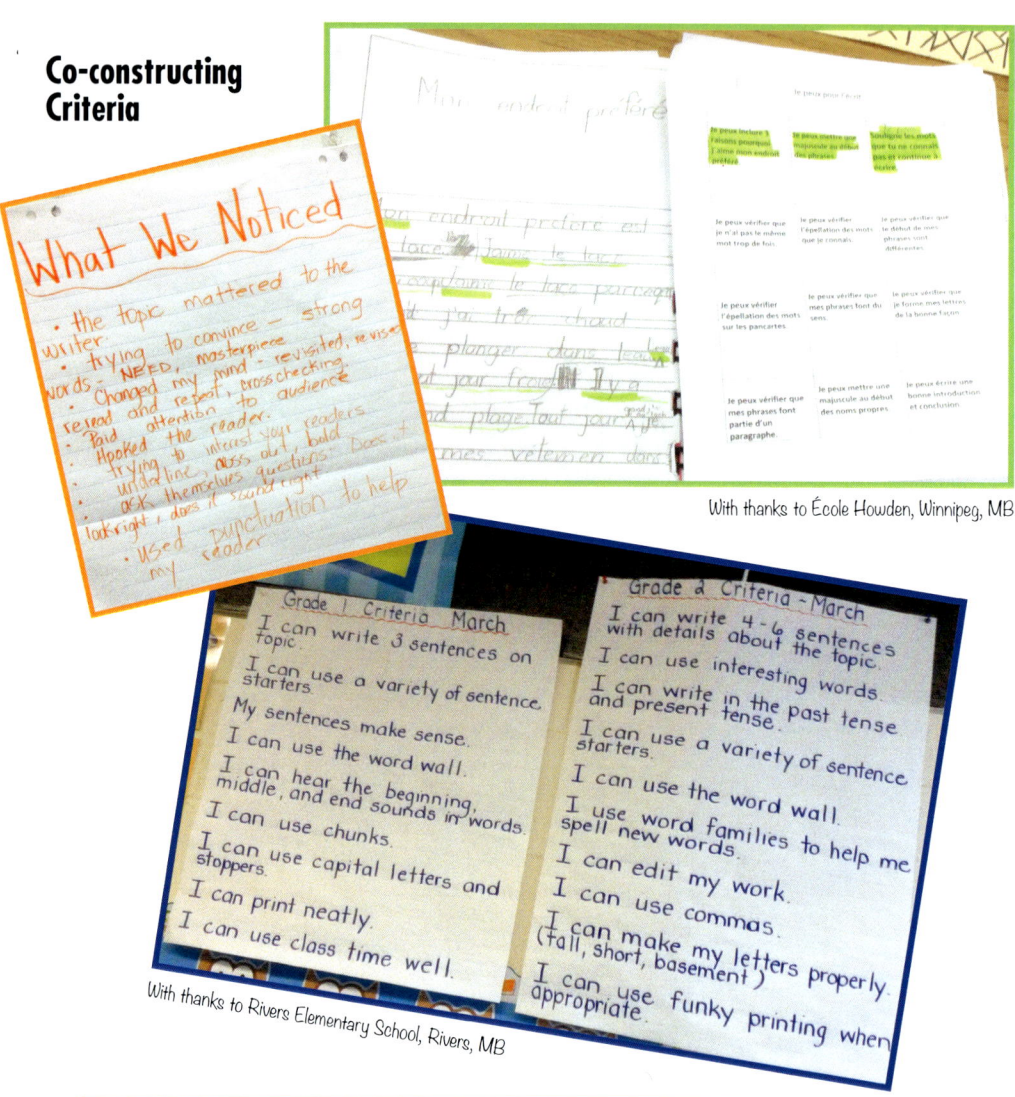

What We Noticed
- the topic mattered to the writer
- trying to convince — strong words, NEED, masterpiece
- Changed my mind - revisited, revised, reread and reshot, crosschecking
- Paid attention to audience
- Hooked the reader.
- trying to interest your readers
- underline, closs out, bold
- ask themselves questions. Does it look right, does it sound right
- Used punctuation to help my reader

With thanks to École Howden, Winnipeg, MB

Grade 1 Criteria March
- I can write 3 sentences on topic.
- I can use a variety of sentence starters.
- My sentences make sense.
- I can use the word wall.
- I can hear the beginning, middle, and end sounds in words.
- I can use chunks.
- I can use capital letters and stoppers.
- I can print neatly.
- I can use class time well.

Grade 2 Criteria - March
- I can write 4-6 sentences with details about the topic.
- I can use interesting words.
- I can write in the past tense and present tense.
- I can use a variety of sentence starters.
- I can use the word wall.
- I use word families to help me spell new words.
- I can edit my work.
- I can use commas.
- I can make my letters properly. (tall, short, basement)
- I can use funky printing when appropriate.

With thanks to Rivers Elementary School, Rivers, MB

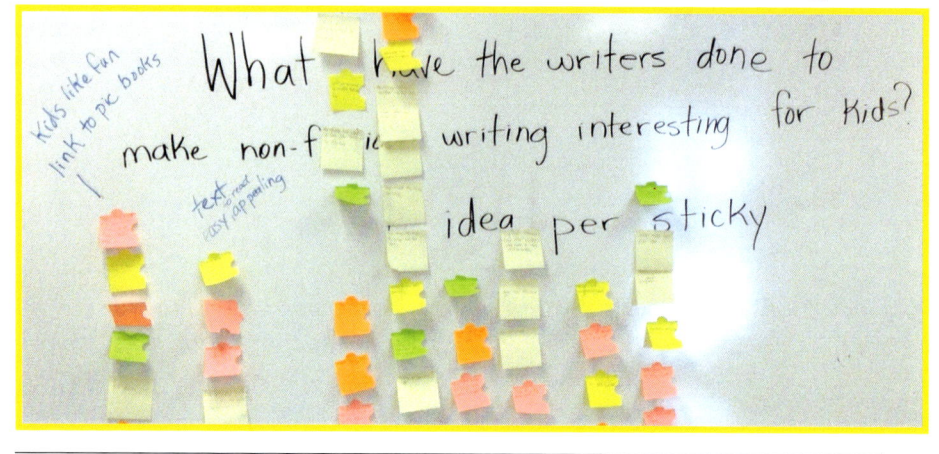

What have the writers done to make non-fiction writing interesting for kids?

idea per sticky

- Kids like fun
- link to pic books
- text read easy appealing

Co-constructing Criteria

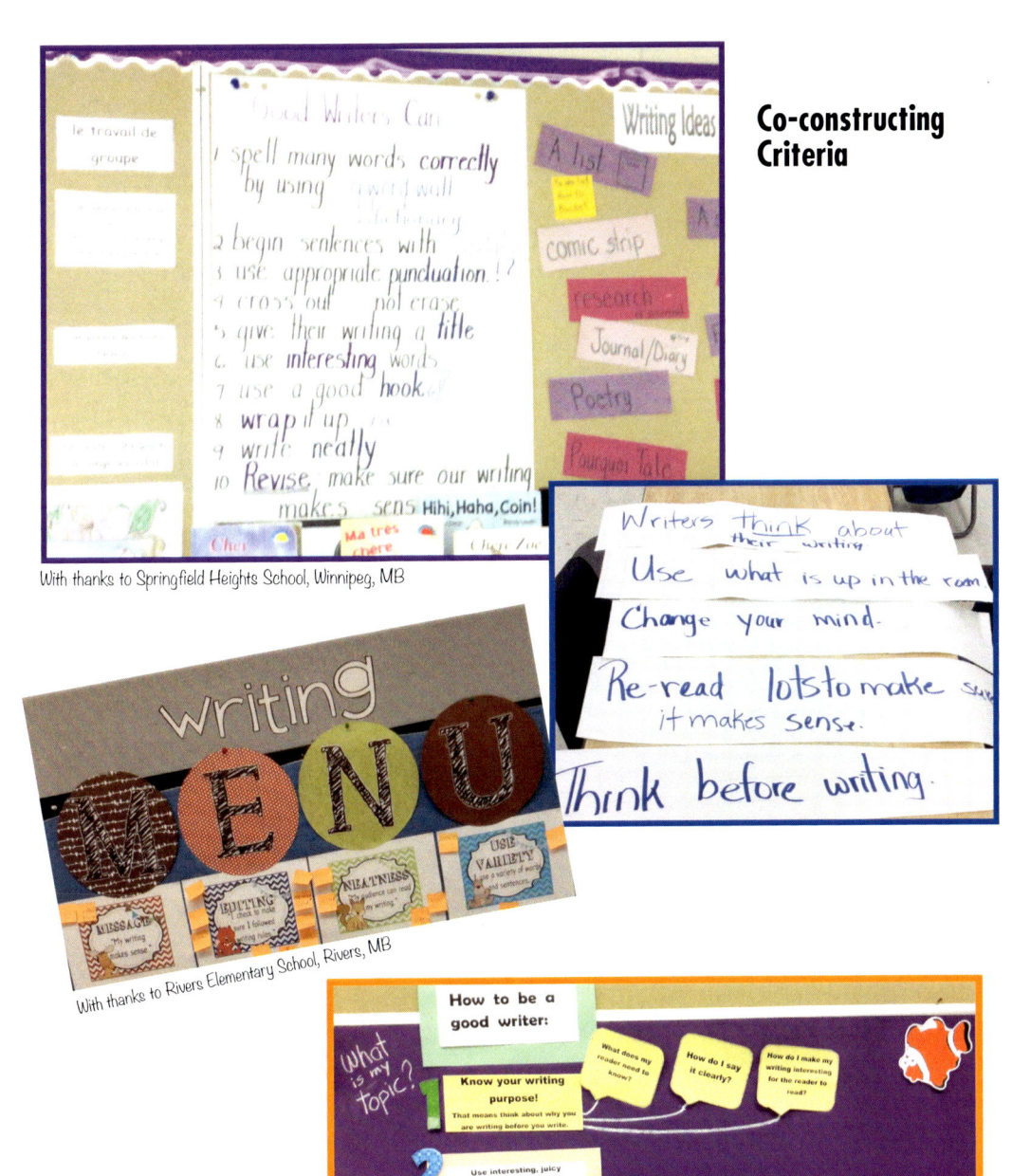

With thanks to Springfield Heights School, Winnipeg, MB

With thanks to Rivers Elementary School, Rivers, MB

With thanks to Springfield Heights School, Winnipeg, MB

Making Writing Instruction Work

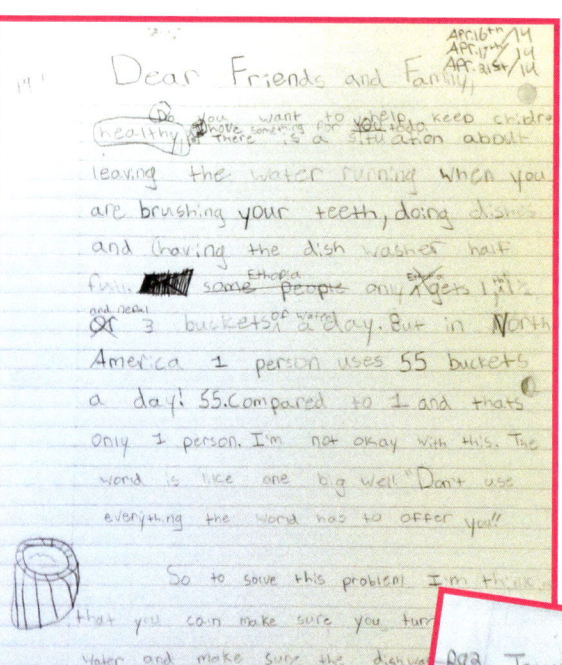

Student Samples

> Dear Friends and Family,
>
> Do you want to help keep children healthy? There is a situation about leaving the water running when you are brushing your teeth, doing dishes and having the dish washer half full. Some people in Ethiopia and Nepal only gets little or 3 buckets of water a day. But in North America 1 person uses 55 buckets a day! 55 compared to 1 and thats only 1 person. I'm not okay with this. The world is like one big well "Don't use everything the world has to offer you!"
>
> So to solve this problem I'm thinking that you can make sure you turn water and make sure the dishwasher for those of you who take maybe take baths for...

> pg 2
> Together we can change the World. Remember one person can make a big difference. I would like that person to be you.
>
> Yours sincerely,

With thanks to Dr. F.W.L. Hamilton School, Winnipeg, MB

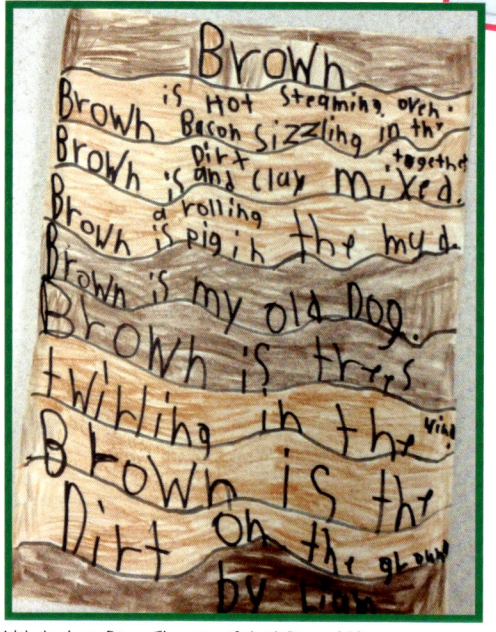

> Brown is Hot steaming oven.
> Brown Bacon sizzling in th' together
> Brown is dirt and clay mixed.
> Brown a rolling
> Brown is pig in the mud.
> Brown is my old Dog.
> Brown is trees twirling in the vine
> Brown is th' Dirt on the ground by...

With thanks to Rivers Elementary School, Rivers, MB

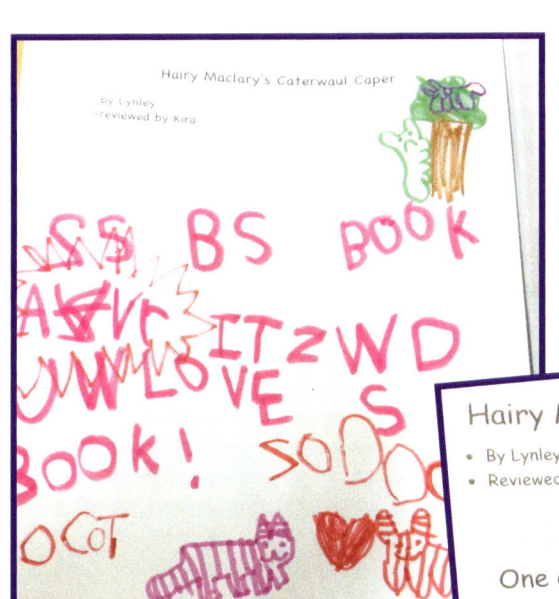

Student Samples

Hairy Maclary's Caterwaul Caper
- By Lynley
- Reviewed by Kira

One of the 25 best books ever! It is so weird. Cats do not like dogs and dogs do not like cats, but in this book a dog helps a cat. You will love this book!

With thanks to Archwood School, Winnipeg, MB

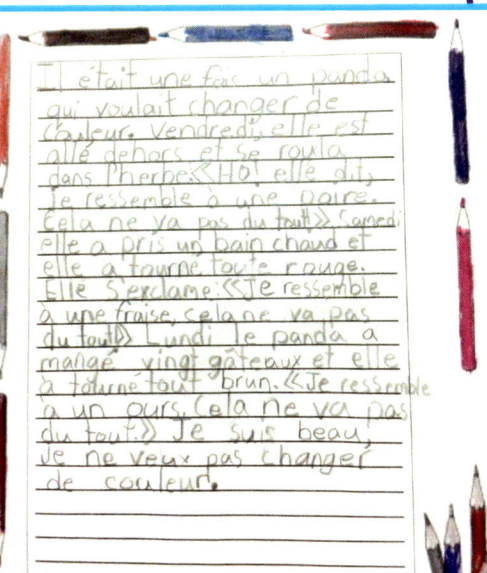

Il était une fois un panda qui voulait changer de couleur. Vendredi, elle est allé dehors et se roula dans l'herbe. «Ho! elle dit, Je ressemble à une poire. Cela ne va pas du tout.» Samedi, elle a pris un bain chaud et elle a tourné toute rouge. Elle s'exclame: «Je ressemble à une fraise, cela ne va pas du tout.» Lundi le panda a mangé vingt gâteaux et elle a tourné tout brun. «Je ressemble à un ours. Cela ne va pas du tout.» Je suis beau, Je ne veux pas changer de couleur.

With thanks to École Howden, Winnipeg, MB

Making Writing Instruction Work

Student Samples

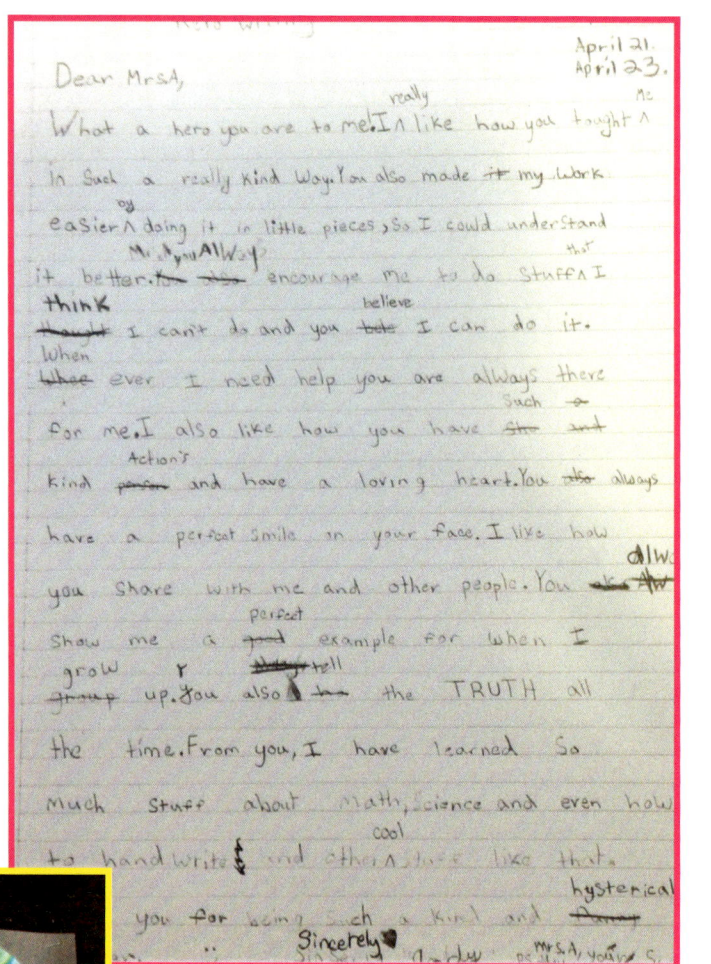

Dear Mrs A,
 April 21.
 April 23.

What a hero you are to me. I really like how you taught me in such a really kind way. You also made by my work easier by doing it in little pieces, so I could understand it better. Ms. A you Allway encourage me to do stuff that I think I can't do and you believe I can do it. When ever I need help you are always there for me. I also like how you have such a kind Action's and have a loving heart. You always have a perfect smile on your face. I like how you share with me and other people. You alwa Show me a perfect example for when I grow r up. You also tell the TRUTH all the time. From you, I have learned so much stuff about Math, Science and even how to handwrite and other cool stuff like that.

hysterical
Sincerely

With thanks to Dr. F.W.L. Hamilton School, Winnipeg, MB

I PROMISE TO TURN OFF THE BY CR

With thanks to Polson School, Winnipeg, MB

I can't wait until grade 6!! I'm going to be in Middle School! Some of my favorite subjects are: GYM and ART. I'm one of the best drawers in the class, and I'm not saying I'm the best. I LOVE sketching. I'm also good at gym, I run fast. I like math to! [NO I DON'T]. But I'm good at it. One more thing I hear is that there's NO RECESS!!! Can we please have at least a 10 minute break. We need to recharge our brains!! Phew, okay so know let's talk about something else, I almost fainted. Now I'm going to tell what I do out of school. I dance hip Hop & Ballet. I know it's kind of weird because Hip Hop and Ballet are totally different dance styles but I like them. I don't think I'm going to go to Ballet next year. I also like gymnastics (I do in school and out of school). I'm good at gymnastics. I can do a cartwheel, one hand cartwheel, handstand, and a front walkover. Also, I can do a bunch of front and back rolls. They are really easy. I also have a sister who is 21 years old. I know, I know, everyone goes "whoa!" because she's so much older than me. I also forgot to tell you that I like to bake, but...I hate to clean up after myself! I hope you're a fun and nice teacher just like Ms. Hererra. I'm looking forward to meeting you!!

With thanks to John Pritchard School, Winnipeg, MB

Making Writing Instruction Work

Chapter 3
Describing Quality

How do you really teach someone to write?

If this is the learning destination, what samples of quality do students need in order to get there?

As a presenter, I often use a quote from Donald Graves (2003), describing the teacher as the "chief learner" in the classroom. In the past, I interpreted this statement to mean that the teacher was learning as much or more about the children as the children were learning about the area of study. Now I see it quite differently. I understand it to mean that the teacher knows more about what quality reading, writing, problem-solving, map-making, researching, experimenting and most importantly, learning, looks like. The teacher is the most expert learner in the community of learners that is the classroom. Teaching really means showing the students what quality could look like and helping them find their pathway to it. As a teacher of writing, I have many options when it comes to showing students pictures of quality.

The Gradual Release of Responsibility

I became a teacher right around the time the gradual release of responsibility model was being documented (Pearson and Gallagher, 1983). And yet, recently I have come to more fully appreciate and understand its importance in the teaching of writing. As someone who spent many years in the Grade 1 classroom, I truly thought I knew all there was to know about gradual release, beginning with modelling, moving toward shared practice, and finally, handing responsibility over to the learner. What I have come to see through the work of many (Routman, 2005; Collins, 2004; Miller, 2012) is that, ironically, we go 'through' the gradual release model way too quickly, even with our youngest learners. We do a perfunctory model so that it doesn't take too much time. We may spend a little more time with a shared write; however, we may only do one, and we may not take time to talk about it. This occurs because we think the students need to get to their own writing. With older elementary, middle school, and high school writers, we sometimes jump right to assigning a writing task, perhaps after only a brief explanation. We hurry because we think our job is to get the students writing, and the more we talk, the less they write. We hurry because we have read that students should be writing daily, and all of this demonstrating, talking, noticing, and writing together takes so much time.

But, it is in the careful, intentional use of the gradual release of responsibility that students learn what quality looks like. Similarly, it is in the careful, intentional use of the gradual release of responsibility that students learn the language of assessment and to monitor, and own, the learning.

Many have learned to refer to this approach as "I do it, We do it, We do it, We do it...You do it" based on the language of Regie Routman's Optimal Learning Model (2005). It has also been described as "For Students, With Students, By Students" and as moving from "Me to We to You." Whatever the language, it is imperative that we slow down and use this process to show students what quality writing looks like.

In the planning stage, I think about where and how I will help students see quality in four main ways. Through sharing samples, modelling, shared writing, and co-constructing criteria, quality writing is no longer a secret known only by a select few. Growth is available to all.

Weaving through these descriptions of quality are hundreds and thousands of words. Words in the form of:

- teacher "think alouds"
- turn and talks between partners
- brainstormed lists of what is noticed in models, shared writes, and samples
- descriptive feedback

Teacher Modelling or Demonstrating

We have a long history of modelling writing in elementary classrooms. It is a growing trend in middle and high school as well, thanks to the work of people such as Penny Kittle (2008) and Kelly Gallagher (2006). Thinking of modelling as a means to describing and showing quality gives it a very specific purpose that I find particularly helpful in making instructional decisions. Returning to the personal letter writing example, it is after reading the initial student letters that I know some of what I want to model for them. My observations as they wrote highlighted the process pieces of which I needed to remind students. While I do not plan exactly what I am going to say, or write the letter the night before and just copy it, I do think of a few key things that I want to communicate in my model. Others emerge in the moment, and I go with that because it is important for students to see a real writer writing for real (Routman, 2005). It is this authenticity that makes it compelling for students to watch, allowing them to see themselves in the picture the teacher is painting of writing.

I keep in mind that while I may be modelling small details about letter writing such as layout, options for the salutation or greeting, and informal endings or, with very young writers, how to spell "dear" (and where it is located on the word wall), this is not my main focus. If I am really modelling what quality writing looks like, I need to focus on the purpose of my letter, my message, and my reader, not simply the mechanics and conventions of writing. If this is a model of quality, it needs to communicate ideas about why we are writing letters. Is it to describe, ask, persuade, thank, comfort, or maybe even to teach? I model how I keep this purpose in mind and make sure that most of my letter is related to it and has a tone suitable for that purpose. I show and talk about how I inject some personal "chat" at the beginning of the letter to make a connection to my reader and infuse the writing with my voice. I decide out loud what to say in the letter and what not to say because my reader already knows it.

Depending upon the grade level and what I saw as students wrote or what I know about them from previous writing experiences, I will also model process. I reread as I write because good writers do that in order to maintain flow, get unstuck, or to hear what their writing sounds like. To make the description of quality even more explicit, I tell the students why I am rereading and how it helps me as a writer.

Notice how I reread to figure out what I want to say next.

See how rereading helps me get unstuck?

Let me reread and see how this sounds. Oh, I don't like how all three sentences start with "and." If I hadn't reread, I would not have seen that.

I also always model revising during the drafting stage because most students seem to think of it as a second, painful step that is best avoided. Demonstration is a picture of what quality writing looks and sounds like — it shows the passion writers have for getting it right for their readers. I want to communicate that revision — changing your mind — is one of the most powerful tools available to a writer. It is not something I am forced to do by my teacher. It is something that I choose to do as a writer who cares about her message and her readers. The description of quality is held in the telling of why we revise, not the act of revision.

I am going to change this word because it won't tell my reader just how grateful I am for her kindness.

I don't know what my opening line is yet so I am going to leave a line as a placeholder and keep writing. It will come to me as I write the letter.

I am going to cross this out because I have changed my mind. I want to say this instead.

Other decisions about what to model are based on what I hear and see in the students. If during the baseline sample they pull out their personal dictionaries for every word, I am going to show how I use the word wall or spell it the best I can, underline the word, and then move on to keep my writing flow going. If the letters all start with "How are you? I am fine." I will model how to make that more interesting for the reader and why it is important to do so.

Another source of feedback comes through chunking the modelling into five to ten minute segments and stopping after each chunk to ask students what they have noticed. As I record their ideas on a chart or sentence strip,

I am listening for what they are noticing and not yet noticing. If I have been rereading and rereading and no one mentions it, I make it even more explicit when I return to the demonstration.

Notice what I did just there. I reread the whole page because I didn't know what to say next. Good writers reread all the time. It helps them know what comes next.

The gradual release of responsibility in writing often, but not always, begins with me writing in front of students. Sometimes I do one model and move on to some shared writing. Sometimes the evidence I see and hear in front of me tells me to do another model. And sometimes, I go back to modelling after I see what the students are doing in their writing. It is not a lockstep process or a recipe. It is an instructional sequence based on the observations, conversations, and partial products occurring in the writing workshop. (See pages 36-40 for examples of Teacher Modelling.)

Shared Writing

Moving along the gradual release of responsibility from Me to We provides another, more student-involved means of support for writers and more opportunities to describe quality. Shared writing, the teacher-led process of writing as a group, is a long-standing component of literacy programming in the early years. It is far too powerful and engaging a strategy to be ignored or eschewed after Grade 3. The amount of teaching, learning, assessing, and relationship building that can occur in fifteen to twenty minutes of shared writing makes it an incredibly valuable and versatile tool in describing quality.

Depending upon what we are writing and our purpose, shared writing may follow the teacher model. Or it may come first. I choose it first when it makes sense — when we are writing in a familiar genre and I want a quick way to remind the students of some things, or when we have had a common experience, such as a speaker or a video, and I know they are ready and able to participate. Because I now view shared writing as another way to show what quality writing looks like, both as a process and as a product, I do it differently than I did when I viewed it simply as one more component of a balanced literacy program.

If it is our first time writing in this way, I tell the students that we are going to write together and that we are exploring how writers can approach this type of writing, letter writing as an example. I tell them that I will be holding the pen and that "the one who holds the pen, holds the power" to make final decisions and keep the writing moving along. I am very much in charge because, again, my purpose is to provide examples of quality writing, and I can't do that if I hand over responsibility at this juncture in the learning sequence. I then proceed to facilitate the writing. I include students, asking them to contribute sentences, to turn and talk, to think about what we are doing that they might try when they get to writing a letter on their own.

As we are writing, I make connections to my models and demonstrations, to the writing criteria we have, and to using the resources available in the room (word wall, charts, books...). I remind them about why we are writing and of our intended audience. I emphasize things we have discovered about good writing in the past and wonder if it works in this situation. I show them through word and deed that writers are always thinking. (See pages 41-43 for examples of Shared Writing.)

Using Student Samples to Describe Quality

Modelling is about using myself as a sample. Saving and sharing student writing samples from one year to the next is another way to deconstruct and illuminate quality writing for students. Some of the ways to use samples include (adapted from *Self-Assessment and Goal Setting*, 2nd Edition, 2011 by Gregory, Cameron & Davies):

- Begin a study of letter writing by reading letters written by students from previous years, another class, or another school. Then ask the students what they noticed or what they learned about letter writing from those writers.

- Share a high-quality sample and ask students what the writer did to make the letter so readable. Chart the responses, creating a list of "What Good Letter Writers Do" or more generally, "What Good Writers Do."

- Share two samples, one of high quality and one of slightly lower quality and ask students what the latter could do to make the letter more interesting for his or her reader and more like the first sample.
- Display three samples, one each of high, medium, and low quality and ask students to consider another sample, inviting them to talk about which of the three samples it is most like and why.

Each interaction with samples of writing makes the picture of what quality really is become increasingly clear. Practice in looking at what other writers have done and assessing these samples in terms of what the writer knows or can do prepares students for looking at their own writing. It shows them that the road to quality writing is paved with many small, imminently do-able steps and not one giant leap.

Co-constructing Criteria

Samples, be they student-generated, a result of shared writes, teacher demonstrations, or a combination of all three, can be used to co-construct criteria about what makes quality writing. The charts or lists described in the first part of the chapter, where students are asked what they noticed in the modelling or what they learned from a particular writer's sample, are really one way to get to the brainstorming step of the four-step process described in *Setting and Using Criteria,* 2nd Edition (Gregory, Cameron, and Davies, 2011a). Other ways to approach the brainstorming include:

- As you model, stop periodically and ask students to tell you what they see and hear you doing. Depending upon the grade and writing speed of the students, they can jot down their thinking, or you can write their ideas on a chart, a sticky note, a sentence strip, or a Smartboard.
- If students have been compiling individual brainstorm lists, have them get together in pairs or small groups and make sure they have each idea written once on a sentence strip.

Collect all the sentence strips or stickies and model how to sort them into categories, the second step in the overall process. Pick up two that go together and place them in a designated spot in the classroom. Choose two more to make another category and find a spot for them. Find and place a third pairing. Students are likely ready to participate at this point. With a partner, they are invited to take a strip to each of the three locations, placing it with those they believe it connects to. Look at each category and decide together what it should be called. The category name becomes the criteria and the strips or stickies are the details that deepen our understanding of the criteria. Rarely does a single word describe a category well enough that all students can understand it. More often a sentence or a phrase does the job.

I make my writing interesting for my reader:

- My first sentence hooks the reader.
- I use "juicy" words.
- I add details.
- My writing is easy to read.

I follow the rules of writing:

- I end my sentences with punctuation and start new sentences with a capital letter.
- Word wall words are correctly spelled.
- I capitalize names.

Moving to the third step — creating and posting a t-chart — creates the space for differentiation. All students will be held to the high expectation of *"Making my writing interesting for my reader,"* although some of them may be focusing on all of the details, others may have two or three specific details they are working to include, and still others may be concentrating on adding interest for the reader for the very first time. The posted criteria gives the community of writers a clear picture of quality and the language to discuss it. See Figure 3.1 and pages 44-45 for examples of using criteria.

Figure 3.1

Our Criteria for Good Writing
Remember the criteria we have made for good writing!

Good Writers Follow the Rules of Writing:

- End with punctuation
- Use a caret (^ or ˅) to add words
- Put capitals on names
- Write some words in CAPITALS
- Cross out when you change your mind
- Use punctuation
- Don't start every sentence with 'I'
- Use interesting words
- Start new paragraphs for new ideas
- Underline words you don't know how to spell
- Start sentences with capitals

Good Writers Think About Their Writing:

- Use what is up in the room
- Change your mind
- Re-read lots to make sure it makes sense
- Think before writing

Good Writers Make it Interesting for the Reader:

- Hook your reader with the first line
- Start sentences in a variety of ways
- Make your writing more interesting for the reader
- Write a closing and make your ending strong
- Use humour if appropriate

With thanks to Rivers Elementary School, Rivers, MB

Co-constructing criteria is a big, time-consuming process. It is not something we do every day, each time we write. I view the fourth step in the process — Add, Revise, Refine — as permission to consider writing workshop as a year-long inquiry. With each experience, each genre, each piece, we are going deeper with the questions:

- What counts in writing?
- What is important in good writing?
- What do good writers do?
- What matters in writing for a reader?

This is not to say that I never co-construct criteria for a specific type of writing, be it free verse poetry, non-fiction reports, or journals. I do. But I also want students to see the bigger picture and to understand that this thing we call writing has a cohesiveness to it; across the genres, there are things that writers do that make it better for their readers. And further, as students of writing, we can notice these things, we can talk and experiment with them, and we can grow in our ability to employ them in the service of our readers.

Chapter 4
Giving Feedback

How do I respond to student writing?

How do I find time to have in-depth writing conferences with each student?

What do I say during writing conferences?

Does my feedback need to be oral? Written?

Writing is risky. As adults, it is a risk that many of us avoid. When asked about writing in their own lives, I have heard teachers say:

- *I don't think I've written anything since university.*
- *I'm really not very good at writing.*
- *I don't like to write.*

As a person for whom writing is an essential activity, one that brings value, clarity, and joy to my life, I want the door to writing wide open for all learners. The messages that we give students about writing in general, and their own writing in particular, matter. With the use of descriptive feedback, we can give messages about writing that will support student writers in the moment and in the future. Messages such as the following can reveal next steps and inspire all students to write again:

- *We are all writers.*
- *Writing is a way we communicate with others and with ourselves.*
- *We can connect to others through writing.*
- *Writing is thinking, not just putting marks on a page.*
- *Writers learn from each other.*

- *We learn by reading what other people write.*
- *Writing and reading go hand in hand.*
- *We can all improve and grow as writers.*
- *Writers work on their craft.*
- *Writing takes effort. Effort leads to better writing.*
- *Writing can be joyful.*

As an educator for whom the principles of assessment for learning are essential to good teaching, I believe that, "To make feedback effective, therefore, teachers must have a good understanding of where the students are, and where they are meant to be — and the more transparent they make this status for the students, the more students can help to get themselves from the points at which they are to the success points, and thus enjoy the fruits of feedback." (Hattie, 2011, p. 115).

Communicating a Growth Mindset

As teachers, we deal in the currency of language. I often joke that I say two million words a day, Monday to Friday from September to June. The care with which I now choose these words has been greatly influenced by Carol Dweck (2006) and Peter Johnston (2012), and it is in the giving of feedback that I am most careful. Through feedback, we communicate messages about success and failure — consciously or unconsciously (Dweck, p.177). Through the word choices I make, it is possible for me to characterize writing as something you are born good at or something that you can get better at with effort over time. Building on Dweck's (2006) descriptions of growth and fixed mindsets, Johnston (2012) describes children's development as either a dynamic-learning frame or a fixed-performance frame. Those with a fixed-performance frame believe that we all have fixed traits that do not change. Either we are good at something or we are not and never will be. Challenging activities are viewed as risky. Conversely, those with a dynamic-learning frame believe in the power of learning and value effort. Challenging activities are viewed as engaging.

Now let's imagine students with each mindset in one of the most challenging settings we have at school — the writing workshop.

Students with a fixed-performance frame:

- *I am not a good writer. I never have been.*
- *I don't know how to write poetry.*
- *Writing is easy for her.*
- *Writing is hard. I am not good at it.*
- *I tried, but I just couldn't do it.*
- *Some people are writers and some are not.*

Students with a dynamic-learning frame:

- *I am growing as a writer.*
- *I made some changes to make my writing better.*
- *I worked hard on this piece.*
- *I tried what Mrs. A. did in her letter.*
- *I talked to my table group and got ideas from them.*

Anything I can do to tip the scales in favour of a growth mindset will better equip my students in their learning journeys.

Using Feedback to Create a Climate for Writing

The first order of business is to create a climate where students are prepared to take the risks necessary to become better writers and to support each other in this endeavour. Feedback, delivered as a celebration of the writing and the writer, can play a critical role in establishing this climate (Routman, 2005). Looking for and describing the strengths in the writing, rather than pointing out errors or weaknesses, shifts the focus from what is missing to what is there, and what is possible. It leaves every writer excited to write, now and in the future.

The language of the feedback comes from the descriptions of quality discussed in the previous chapter and emerges directly from the learning destination. It is found in the models, the shared writes, the student samples, and the criteria for what good writers do. As the teacher models writing a book review, you might hear:

- *I am thinking of a great first sentence because writers hook their readers with their opening line.*
- *I am going to reread this part to see if I like how it sounds.*
- *I am going to cross out "said" and use a "juicier," more interesting word.*
- *I need to tell my readers something really interesting about the book so that they will want to read it.*
- *Too many of my sentences are starting with "And." I am going to change that because it will not be very interesting for my reader.*

As we move along the gradual release of responsibility, the shared writing might sound like this:

Teacher: *I think our first sentence is going to hook our readers.*

Student: *We could change our mind and cross out "nice" and use a more interesting word.*

Student: *I think the sentence should end with an exclamation mark.*

Teacher: *Who can get us started? Rereading what we have will help.*

Student: *I don't think we should tell how the book ends. No spoilers!*

Based on samples of the genre, the teacher models, and the shared writes, criteria emerge. Because it grows naturally from the samples of quality, the language is very familiar. Building on all the language that has come before, descriptive feedback for student poems might look and sound like Figure 4.1.

Figure 4.1

Bunnies Bunnies hop And are just like hares. Bunnies have Big fat ears. Bunnies are fluffy. Bunnies are soft Bunnies are so cute Bunnies can be brown and black And white. Bunnies have two big teeth. Do you have a bunny? Bunnies live in the forest. (by a Grade 1 poet)	**Feedback I might give:** It looks like a poem: • You have white space. • You change lines often. • Your poem is centred on the page. It sounds like a free verse poem: • It doesn't rhyme. • You have used words to describe the bunny. • Your line breaks make it sound like a poem.

When this feedback is given to a student publicly as they sit in the Author's Chair next to you, it becomes a celebration, a way of describing the wonderful things this writer is doing and a way of reminding all the other writers of what they might do. It makes the writing joyful, a cause for celebration. It is a way of delivering many of the messages about writing listed above, while establishing that this is a safe place in which to learn the craft.

Because chances are that many of the writers may need the same feedback, it is also a very efficient way to have conferences. We can reach more than one writer at a time. This buys us the time to really slow things down for our learners and lavish them with feedback that describes in detail the things they are doing that meet criteria, creating a setting where writing is celebrated and writers are continually reminded of what good writers do.

Using Feedback to Teach Self- and Peer Assessment

Giving feedback in this public way models for the students how we treat another's work, the language we use, and the things we notice. These public conferences are in fact yet another model, another loop in the gradual release of responsibility, this time modelling assessment. As the teacher gives feedback in this public and oral format, many goals are being met:

- We are coming together as a community of writers.
- The student receiving the feedback is hearing confirmation about criteria he or she has met and evidence from the writing that proves this.
- The other writers listening in are being reminded of the criteria for good writing and encouraged to think about it in relation to their own writing.
- All writers are experiencing confirmation of the learning destination, further evidence of what quality looks and sounds like when writing.
- All writers are seeing and hearing that having your writing shared publicly is a safe, positive, joyful, and valuable learning experience.
- All writers are learning the language of assessment as they hear the teacher model it.

Improving our Ability to Give Feedback

Like all valuable skills, giving feedback benefits from practice. If the goal is to celebrate a writer and a piece of writing in the moment in front of the class, a couple of intermediary steps will build your confidence.

Practice with Colleagues

- Choose a piece of writing from your student samples. With a partner or a team, take turns describing what the writer is able to do.

- Focus on what is there, not what is missing.
- Read the piece aloud, with only one of you looking at the paper. It can be easier to focus on what is working when we do not see the writing.

Make Notes

- Look at some brief writing samples on your own in advance of sharing publicly with the students.
- On a sticky note, write three to five things you notice the writer doing.
- Use the notes to give descriptive feedback to a writer in a public conference.

Co-teach with a Colleague

- Invite a colleague to observe during a time when you are giving feedback publicly.
- Ask your colleague to script what you say. Look at the transcript and consider the language you are using. Is it having the desired impact? What words do you like the sound of? What might you consider changing?
- Observe a colleague who is more experienced in giving descriptive feedback. Script his or her language. What do you hear that could work for you? How might you adapt this language to fit your style?

You may be wondering about all of this focus on celebrating the strengths of the writing and the writer. "When," you might be asking yourself, "do you point out next steps?" How will my students learn to write well if I don't show them what they are doing wrong?" The combined powers of celebration, knowing where you are going, and what quality looks like, can move writers a long way. It is not that we must never name next steps, but rather that we do so judiciously, without overwhelming students with all that is lacking and must be done to improve.

The decision about when to include next steps for a student comes down to the purpose of the feedback and the knowledge of individual students. If my purpose is to build a classroom community where all see themselves as writers and are willing to make their writing and their thinking public, then I may decide to focus on celebrating and describing what is present in the writing or in the writing process. Next steps are implied and put on the table as I make decisions about what to focus on and what to model or include in the shared writing. When the writing community is well established, I may decide to introduce the language of "A next step for you might be..." or "Next time you could try...." This might happen in a public conference, if I think the student is ready for that and others would benefit. It could also take place in a one-to-one conversation.

Individual Writing Conferences and Small Group Instruction

There will be times when you decide to have individual conferences. Asking yourself two questions, in the order given, can help choose among the available instructional options:

- What is my purpose at this moment in the instructional sequence?
  - Why I am doing this?
- Who is the audience?
  - Is it all my students, some of them, or one of them?

If I want to show students how to choose a topic with a specific focus and my observations tell me that many of them need this, I am going to choose to begin with a public conference followed by a debrief of what went on:

- *Writers, what did you hear me ask that you could ask yourself?*
- *What did you learn about starting a book review?*

I may have them turn and talk with a partner about what they are going to write and then send off those who are ready to write. Those wanting to talk to me remain behind. I can have quick one-to-one discussions with them, thereby reducing the number of students who require an individual conversation. After they have been writing for some time, I will go from student to student, giving just-in-time feedback.

To the reluctant writer who got right down to it, I might say:

You left a blank for the title to come back to later. Good writers do that and keep themselves writing. Your first sentence really hooked me. Keep going, I can't wait to see what comes next.

To the risk-averse writer who likes to know how to spell everything correctly, I might say:

You copied the title from the cover of the book. Writers use the resources in the room. I noticed you checking words on the word wall, and in this word you wrote down all the sounds you heard. That is what good writers do. They also spell a word as best they can and underline it to say, "I am not sure about this, but I will check it later." And then they keep themselves writing.

To the writer who doesn't like to revise and claims to love all first drafts as written, I might say:

I noticed that you crossed out a word and changed your mind. That shows what a thinking writer you are and that you really care about your reader.

Generally I follow these individual "on the fly" conferences with public conferences, in which I give descriptive feedback related to our criteria and the conversations we have had as a result of my modelling and our shared writes. Like many teachers, I am an inveterate list maker, keeping track of whose work has been read aloud and celebrated, who might be ready to talk with me publicly about a next step, and who is putting the things I am modelling into practice. Some of this can be shared with students as group feedback. If I have been modelling using cross-outs and carets to revise, explaining how poetry looks different on a page than prose, or starting my lines in a different way, this is what I look for when I collect student work. The next day, I share some feedback with the whole group, based on a checklist I made as I read. See Figure 4.2 on page 68.

Figure 4.2

Feedback Checklist			
Name	Looks like a poem	Showed evidence of revision in draft	Began lines in different ways

Writers, as I was reading your book reviews, I noticed that all of you are thinking about hooking your reader right from the first line. I noticed that most of you are trying the strategy of underlining words you are unsure of how to spell so that you can keep yourself writing. I also saw that very few of you are changing your mind about what you want to say and showing that by crossing out and adding in something new. Good writers reread as they go to make sure that the writing is saying exactly what they want it to.

My next instructional step would be to model what I want them to be doing more of — in this case, rereading and revising as they write. Students would then return to their own writing, practising what has been modelled and using the feedback to improve their writing. At this point in the process, it is all about feedback related to the learning destination and the criteria. This focus makes it clear to me what to look for and what to comment on as I read student writing. It prevents me from overwhelming students with feedback on everything I know about writing all at once. It gives me permission to refrain from putting a mark on what is not yet ready to be evaluated. It honours the value of practice time and establishes the rhythm I want for writing workshop…practice, practice, practice…showtime.

Giving descriptive feedback that is linked to the learning destination and the samples of quality supports learners in understanding where they are in relation to those targets. It also gives them the language to both self- and peer assess. Now they are ready for opportunities to use those newly developed skills.

Chapter 5
Involving Students in Self- and Peer Assessment

How can I possibly read all of that writing and mark it?

How do you teach students to peer edit?

We created a writing continuum but now what?

It happened in May. I was co-teaching in a Kindergarten class, and I was with a group of seven or eight students seated in front of the first three samples of our writing continuum. Each was holding a piece of his or her own writing and looking at the samples on the wall. One of the boys got up to leave. "Let's all stay with the group," I reminded him. His response was the one that taught me once and for all to listen first, remind later. "I just noticed that mine only has a picture and the one up on the wall has a picture and words. I'm not done. I need to finish it."

And he did.

Involving Students in Assessment

Begin with Language

From the moment we begin noticing what counts in writing a book review or a free verse poem, we are involving students in the assessment process. When we ask students to turn and talk about what they noticed the teacher do in the modelling or what they learned from the student writer whose writing we have just read, they are practising the language of assessment. The language I use with students very quickly becomes the language they use with each other. I intentionally plant the words and phrases they will need to give themselves and each other worthwhile descriptive feedback in a positive, respectful, appreciative, and joyful way.

As I write in front of students, I stop periodically and ask, "What did you notice me do or say that you could try when you write?" Almost immediately, students begin their conversations with, "I noticed..." without anyone directing them to do so. Their responses are recorded on a chart that we add to over the course of several days. As we do a shared write, I begin to model how to give feedback using the criteria.

Look at this, boys and girls. I noticed that we have a hook at the beginning to really grab our readers' attention, just like it says on the chart.

I notice that we have used some "juicy" words like ....

Again, I draw their attention to the brainstormed list of what counts in good writing.

With a partner, please find one thing from the chart that you notice from the list in our shared write and come and show me where it is in the writing.

In this way we practise finding evidence of the criteria in our writing. Just like writing itself, self-assessment must be modelled again and again. It is much easier for students to start with writing that is not their own. Therefore, I begin with my own demonstrations, shared writes, and/or writing from other years or other classes with names removed. After considerable practice together, I model again how I can look at my own writing and describe two things I notice from the criteria list. I ask them to do the same. Peer assessment is a natural next step, as students can share what they notice about their own work or that of a partner. What has come before ensures that the spirit and language of descriptive feedback protects and supports each learner.

Using Criteria

Posting criteria is an important step, but if we stop there our students miss out on the full potential this strategy offers. The students need to own the criteria, and they can only own it if they are responsible for using it in purposeful ways.

Finding Evidence of Criteria

Through modelling and shared practice, we can teach students to show evidence of what good writers do (writing criteria) in their own and each other's work. I begin with my own writing on the chart stand and show how I can underline with a yellow marker to show evidence that I think while I write.

Depending upon student response to the demonstration, I might decide to involve them in further practice with one of our shared writes, or I might release them to try it with their own writing, working with a partner. In the whole-group discussion that follows, I choose various partners to share what they have found. I intentionally select the aspect of writing or the student I believe needs to be validated or affirmed at this moment. I also purposefully choose the order in which students will share, generally beginning with something everyone has noticed or discovered and moving up to more sophisticated or higher levels of thinking. In this way, every student sees himself/herself in the picture, and every student sees a next step.

Depending upon the age and experience of the writers and my observations as we move forward, I decide when they are ready to add more criteria, when they need more instruction about a particular aspect in the criteria, or even when the criteria needs to be revised to better meet our needs.

Next Steps or Goal Setting

The power of public conferences and positive descriptive feedback is far-reaching. Without me ever saying specifically to a writer, "You should do this too," most students will try one or more of the things emphasized in the feedback cycle. As I work to build the community of writers, I rely on this power. Once it is well established, I move to model how we can give descriptive feedback about what we notice from the criteria of what good writers do and add, "Next time you might try...." As this process is modelled and explored, students learn to give themselves and their peers feedback and suggest a goal for improvement.

"I can" Statements

Another way to work with criteria is to write "I can" statements. When I do this, like most instructional decisions, depends upon my purpose. At the end of a unit of study, I might ask students to help me make a list of the things I should be able to expect in their published book reviews, free verse, expert writing, or animal reports. See pictures on pages 44-45.

These statements can be used in self- and peer assessment in a variety of ways:

- Choose five of the "I can" statements and ask students to show evidence of them in their writing.
- Create a chart for students to use in self- or peer assessment based on criteria or "I can" statements (see Figure 5.1).
- Include a "Please Notice" or "Next Time Try" column (adapted from Gregory et al., 2011a).

Figure 5.1

"I can" Statements/Criteria	Met	Not Yet Met
I can hook my reader		
I can add details to make my writing more interesting.		

Using Student Samples to Self- and Peer Assess

As described in Chapter 2, samples provide a description of quality – a picture of what success can look like. When I am the model, no matter how hard I try, I cannot be as close to student writing as another student can. These "near samples" can illustrate next steps in a clear and concrete way, showing the writer a small, manageable next step rather than the very large and vague step of "becoming a better writer." Here samples are used again, this time as a way to involve students in self-assessment (Gregory et al., 2011b).

Using One Sample

Display one sample and ask students to describe what they notice as you create a list. To be even more explicit, use arrows to show exactly where each characteristic occurs in the piece.

What did this writer do?

How is your writing similar to this sample?

Using Two Samples

Begin with one sample, as in the example above. Add in a second sample of slightly higher quality, based on the criteria you are using or working toward with students, and ask students to respond to the following questions:

What did the second writer do that the first one did not?

Which sample is your writing most like?

Through questioning and paraphrasing, guide students in seeing the difference between the samples. I use this approach for a variety of purposes:

- To show students another way we can learn from other writers.
- To illustrate that we can learn from all writers, not only the teacher.
- To show students how we can grow as writers by looking at two samples and comparing the differences.
- To move a small or large group forward where Sample One reflects where many students are and Sample Two is a possible next step.

Using Multiple Samples

A collection of samples reflecting the range of writers in your class allows you to teach students how to compare their own writing to the samples and find the closest match. Leading with this strategy provides the support students need to have when looking at the writing they care most about — their own. Again, this work needs to be modelled with students who are ready to do this with you publicly.

I ask for permission in private, describing what will happen and what I will say. If a student is reluctant, I ask another. After observing it once, many students are willing to volunteer because they see and hear the respectful language and the emphasis on what is present, not absent, in the writing.

Once students are able to find the range of samples (I encourage them to see that they might be working in a two to three sample range) that their piece is most closely connected to and why, it is a simple matter for most to see that "I am here and my next step is...." This is what the many descriptions of quality, the modelling, the shared experiences, and the opportunities for independent practice have all been about. An independent, self-regulating writer can now know what quality looks like, the degree to which it exists in his or her own writing, and the changes required to meet more of the criteria. Involving students in self- and peer assessment sets them on the path to becoming self-monitoring and self-regulating learners — learners who know where they are, where they are headed, and what they must do to close the gap.

Chapter 6
Planning for Success

Where do I start?

How do I find the time?

How can I do this and write report cards too?

Begin with the End in Mind

We need to know where we are going. As teachers we must understand and communicate not only where we are going, but why it matters and how we will know when we get there. If we don't know, then no one will.

The easy answer is the curriculum. The paradox is that the curriculum is not enough. The bigger, richer, more profound answer is the curriculum in the hands of a reflective, skilled professional who knows her audience, the students in front of her right now, and her purpose – to inspire students to understand and use the power of written communication.

To fully teach the curriculum, we need to do more than teach genres for the sake of knowing about genres. We need to teach in such a way that our students see the value in knowing how to write persuasively, which is different than knowing how to write a book review. We need to teach in ways that allow our students to see that we learn and follow the conventions of writing, not simply because they are rules, but because they make it possible to write with greater clarity and impact for our readers.

We need to help students connect the dots, and we need to do it in a way that is time efficient, sustainable, and connected to the bigger picture of what we do as teachers. In *Making Classroom Assessment Work* (Davies, 2000, 2011), a four-step planning frame is presented that supports us in doing all of these things.

The Assessment Plan

Three of the four sections of the assessment plan have already been discussed in previous chapters: the learning destination, possible evidence, and descriptions of quality. The final quadrant describes the profile of the writer who fully meets expectations for this unit of study. In its entirety it looks like Figure 6.1:

Figure 6.1

Grade 5 Fur Trade Writing

Learning Destination **Know:** • The conventions of non-fiction report writing **Understand:** • The purpose of this genre is to communicate learning to others. • Making writing interesting in expository writing is done differently than in narrative writing. **Do:** • Think and plan before beginning research. • Research and write on a topic from the Fur Trade following co-constructed criteria. • Write about one or more topics for a class book about the Fur Trade. • Work collaboratively with a partner on one section of the book. **Say:** • Be able to articulate the purpose and audience for this inquiry.	**Evidence We Could Collect** **Conversations:** • Conference with pairs: when plan is complete, when research is done, when writing draft is complete. • Create exit slips after each model or shared practice. What do you know about this part of the process? What is the muddiest point? • Record highlights after Turn and Talks. • Ask each student to write or describe the purpose and audience of the project. **Observations:** • Collect anecdotal records on these focus questions: • Has the team written meaningful research questions? • Are the students able to write jot notes that meet the criteria? What do they still need to understand? • When draft writing is reviewed early in the process, make a checklist of key things to look for: writing in own words, evidence of revision and rereading, using criteria as a guide. **Products:** • Jot notes • Plan • Draft writing • Published text
Descriptions of Quality **(Models/Samples/Frontloading)** • Model and do shared writes of reading non-fiction text, taking jot notes, turning notes into writing, writing a bibliography. • Show student samples of jot notes and writing. • Co-construct criteria for taking jot notes. • Co-construct criteria for what counts in non-fiction reports. • Co-construct criteria for working together if it does not exist.	**Evaluation** **(What defines meeting expectations?)** • Jot notes meet criteria. • Final draft fully meets criteria. • Student can communicate about the purpose and the audience. • Student can identify elements of non-fiction report writing.

Notice the connectedness of this plan. In the first quadrant, I have laid out the learning destination in both big ideas and specifics. The second quadrant describes the conversations, observations, and products that the students and I will need to collect to show evidence of where they are in relation to that target. The descriptions of quality are the specific teaching moves that will become my instructional sequence. I do not necessarily know the specific order they will be in. For example, often I begin with a demonstration, but sometimes a shared write is the best jumping off point. The decision is made depending upon my purpose and where the students are.

The final quadrant describes what the evidence for a student who fully meets expectations at the end of the unit of study will look and sound like. It reflects the information from the first three boxes and is very reminiscent of the quadrant describing the learning destination, as it should be if it is truly reflecting the writer's ability to hit the intended target. Quadrants one and four also contribute language that can be used in writing report card comments — identifying strengths, challenges, and next steps. See Appendix B for more examples of assessment plans.

With these four steps, I am ready for the next four to eight weeks of writing instruction. My planning cannot be done "minute-by-minute" because I need to see what my students do at instructionally significant moments along the way. Following their lead, I use my professional judgment, along with the plan I have mapped out, to decide what comes next.

Conclusion

The conclusions I draw from this work are based on the conversations, observations, and products I have collected from the learners — children and adults alike — I work with. The evidence of the success of this approach to teaching writing is found in this triangulated evidence. See more student samples, both in draft and published form, on pages 46-48.

Conversations

Grade 3 student when asked what was different about the way they were learning to write this year: *"We are using three easy steps: I do it, We do it, You do it... instead of ten hard steps."*

Grade 1 student pointing to the draft copy of his poem: *"I like how it sounds with the line break here."*

Teacher: *"Can you read me your book review?"*
Kindergarten student with educational assistant sitting next to him: *"Funny book"* (as he pointed to three smiling faces which turned out to be his family as they read the book).

Grade 8 student after participating in a shared write about trash islands in our oceans: *"We have to do something about this. We have to write to more people."*

Observations

On Day Three of the Writer's Workshop, when I released Kindergarten students to begin writing their book reviews, they ran to their seats to get started. (This was excitement, not lack of classroom management!)

When the Grade 1s went to write, no one said, *"I don't know what to write."*

All Grade 5 students began writing to next year's teachers immediately, including those the teacher reported as the most reluctant writers in the room.

At no time during the twenty minutes of writing did I have a "tail" of students following me. All students kept themselves writing.

All Grade 8 students started their letters on the topic of what we can do to look after our world better. No comments were made about not knowing what to do or what to write. At the end of the week, one of the Grade 8 students said to the principal, *"We need to do something about this issue. It can't just stop here."*

Products

The best evidence is collected over time. This first sample comes from a Grade 1 writer.

Figure 7.1

I'm a Dog Expert
By Kaitlin

I'm perfect at playing with my dog. It's like we're related. Her name is Sasha. I've been playing with her since I was little. She is the best dog ever because she give me kisses! I take pride in being a dog expert.

With thanks to John Pritchard School, Winnipeg, MB

Here she is again one year later…

Figure 7.2

April 10, 2015

Dear Grade 0 Class,

    I am warning you! Global warming is taking over and it is affecting the polar bears. Do you know what global warming is? Global warming is when the air in the sky gets warmer and warmer. Polar bears are dying because icebergs are getting farther and farther apart. Since the air is really warm, it breaks the ice up. They are drowning because the ice floes are too far apart. This is **absolutely horrific**.

    We can help save the polar bears. We can do something about this problem. Please tell your parents to stop smoking, stop working at factories, and NEVER leave their cars running when they are idling. Please tell your friends and family to wear more clothes if they are cold instead of making a fire. This will help stop polluting and making the air hot.

    Don't worry; this is not the end of our solutions. If you have any more ideas of how you can help, please ask your teacher to contact Mrs. P. We will be happy to listen to your ideas.

From your friend,

Kaitlin

With thanks to John Pritchard School, Winnipeg, MB

Imagine this writer in another year. Imagine her in five years after spending her time in elementary school with teachers committed to identifying a clear learning destination, many descriptions of quality, and descriptive feedback. Imagine her being one of many students involved in collecting evidence of his/her own learning and setting goals for the future. Imagine her in high school, after leaving the K–8 setting, where teachers know that students benefit from this approach to writing instruction every bit as much as they do in elementary school. Just imagine.

I end this book as I began it...with one last question...

How often do I need to do this?

And one final response...

Only when you want quality writing.

Appendix A:
Learning Destinations

- Kindergarten Book Reviews
- Grade 1/2 Combined Class 6 Things You Should Know About My Community
- Grade 2 Free Verse Poetry
- Grade 5 ELA and Social Studies Fur Trade Unit of Study

Kindergarten Book Reviews

Learning Destination (What we want students to Know, Understand, and Do)

Bold: Big ideas

Bullet Points: Outcomes from Manitoba Kindergarten curriculum and author's additions (in italics)

Writers and readers talk and write to share what they know and feel with others:
- know that ideas expressed in oral language can be drawn and recorded
- tell and draw stories about self, *specifically a book they like*
- make connections between texts and personal experiences
- represent and share information and ideas
- talk about personal experiences with books
- share experiences, feelings, and thoughts
- express preferences for favourite texts
- share information and ideas about a topic of personal interest
- share information and ideas with a group
- relate aspects of stories to personal feelings and experiences
- contribute to group stories
- *write for a real audience and purpose*

Writers use what they know about sounds, letters, words, and pictures to tell their story for their readers:
- recognize that print is organized from top to bottom and left to right, recognize that letters represent sounds, and match sounds with print
- group ideas and information to make sense
- develop a sense of story
- experiment with letters, sounds, words, and word patterns
- create original texts to communicate and demonstrate understanding
- form recognizable letters

- describe and enhance own drawings, stories, and writing using images and sounds
- use drawings and labels to express ideas, feelings, and information
- connect sounds with letters in words
- recognize own name, upper and lower case letters, familiar logos, and periods
- *use cross-outs to change mind*

Writers learn from each other and support each other:
- demonstrate active listening and viewing skills and strategies, *specifically noticing what good writers do*
- participate in cooperative group activities
- demonstrate attentiveness during group activities
- find ways to be helpful to others and use group process
- *participate in scaffolded conversations and public conferences*

Learning Destination for Kindergarten Book Reviews

KNOW:
- What we say we can write down.

UNDERSTAND:
- Writers and readers use what they know about sounds, letters, words, and pictures to tell their story for their readers and to keep themselves writing.
- Writers and readers learn from each other and support each other.

DO:
- Participate in several shared writes about book reviews.
- Write and draw about a book.

SAY:
- Students will be able to tell what they are writing and for whom they are writing.

6 Things You Should Know About My Community*
Grade 1

Big Ideas in Bold: These are the ideas I will focus on with the students:
- Grade 1 outcomes from Manitoba curriculum

English Language Arts

Writers and readers talk and write to share what they know and feel with others:
- listen to and acknowledge experiences and feelings shared by others
- choose to read and write with and for others
- describe new experiences and ideas
- connect new experiences and information with prior knowledge
- share feelings and moods evoked by oral, literary, and media texts
- tell, draw, and write about self and family
- participate in shared listening, reading, and viewing experiences using texts from a variety of forms, genres, and cultural traditions

Writers and readers use what they know about sounds, letters, words, and pictures to tell their story for their readers and to keep themselves writing:
- experiment with parts of words, word combinations, and word patterns for a variety of purposes
- use sound-symbol relationships and visual memory to spell familiar words
- capitalize the first letters of names, the beginnings of statements, and the pronoun "I"
- use periods
- experiment with words and sentence patterns using specific structures

Writers and readers learn from each other and support each other:
- demonstrate active listening and viewing skills and strategies
- work in cooperative and collaborative partnerships and groups
- take turns sharing information and ideas
- help others and ask others for help
- identify and assume roles necessary for maintenance of group process

*Adapted from ESPN magazine

Writers can choose to write in different ways or forms depending upon their purpose and audience:
- use a variety of forms to express and explore familiar events, ideas, and information
- recognize different forms and genres of oral, literary, and media texts
- appreciate repetition, rhyme, and rhythm in shared language experiences
- create original texts to communicate and demonstrate understanding of forms and techniques

Writers think about their writing and making it clear and interesting for themselves and their readers:
- demonstrate interest in and suggest enhancements for own and others' work
- group and sort ideas and information to make sense
- rephrase and represent to clarify ideas
- strive for consistency in letter size and shape
- print letters legibly from left to right horizontally, using lines on a page as a guide
- check for completeness of work and add details and enhancements

Social Studies

When we write as researchers we can use strategies to communicate our thinking and learning:
- gather information from oral, visual, material, print, or electronic sources
- present information and ideas orally, visually, concretely, or electronically
- express reasons for their ideas and opinions
- use comparison in investigations
- use information or observation to form opinions
- categorize information using selected criteria

continued on next page

Grade 1 Learning Destination

KNOW:
- One form writers can write in is a "6 Things" format.
- Sometimes writers write to teach their readers and to show what they know.

UNDERSTAND:
- Writers and readers use what they know about sounds, letters, words, and pictures to tell their story for their readers and to keep themselves writing.
- Writers think about their writing and making it clear and interesting for themselves and their readers.
- Writers and readers learn from each other and support each other.

DO:
- Write in the "6 Things" format following the co-constructed criteria.
- Show evidence of rereading and revision.

SAY:
- Students will be able to tell what they are writing and for whom they are writing.

6 Things You Should Know About My Community*
Grade 2

Big Ideas in Bold : These are the ideas I will focus on with the students:
- Grade 2 outcomes from Manitoba curriculum

English Language Arts

Writers and readers talk and write to share what they know and feel with others:
- make and talk about personal observations
- ask for others' ideas and observations to help discover and explore personal understanding.
- express preferences for a variety of oral, literary, and media texts
- develop a sense of self as reader, writer, and illustrator
- connect new information, ideas, and experiences with prior knowledge and experiences
- explain new experiences and understanding
- choose to engage in a variety of shared and independent listening, reading, and viewing experiences using texts from a variety of forms
- generate and contribute ideas on particular topics for oral, written, and visual texts
- share own stories and creations with peers and respond to questions or comments
- connect situations portrayed in oral, literary, and media texts to personal experiences

Writers and readers learn from each other and support each other:
- participate in shared language experiences to celebrate individual and class achievement
- work in a variety of cooperative and collaborative partnership and group structures
- contribute related ideas and information in whole-class and small-group activities
- acknowledge achievements of others
- rehearse roles and responsibilities in group process by helping others and asking others for help

*Adapted from ESPN magazine

continued on next page

Writers can choose to write in different ways or forms depending upon their purpose and audience.
- use a variety of forms to organize and give meaning to familiar experiences, ideas, and information
- create original texts to communicate and demonstrate understanding of forms and techniques
- recognize that information and ideas can be expressed in a variety of forms and genres
- use a variety of forms for particular audiences and purposes
- demonstrate interest in the sounds of words and word combinations in pattern books, poems, songs, and oral and visual presentations

Writers think about their writing and making it clear and interesting for themselves and their readers:
- arrange ideas and information to make sense
- order ideas to create a beginning, middle, and end in own oral, written, and visual texts
- revise illustrations and representations by adding or deleting words and details to make sense
- form letters and words of consistent size and shape
- print legibly using correct letter formation and spacing
- experiment with words and simple sentence patterns to enhance communication forms
- combine illustrations and written texts to express ideas, feelings, and information
- check work for beginning, middle, and end
- spell familiar words using a variety of strategies
- use periods and question marks as end punctuation

Social Studies
When we write as researchers we can use strategies to communicate our thinking and learning:
- select information from oral, visual, material, print, or electronic sources
- present information and ideas orally, visually, concretely, or electronically
- express reasons for their ideas and opinions
- formulate questions for research
- use information or observation to form opinions
- organize and record information using visual organizers

Grade 2 Learning Destination
KNOW:
- One form writers can write in is a "6 Things" format.
- Sometimes writers write to teach their readers and to show what they know.

UNDERSTAND:
- Writers and readers use what they know about sounds, letters, words, and pictures to tell their story for their readers and to keep themselves writing.
- Writers think about their writing and making it clear and interesting for themselves and their readers.
- Writers and readers learn from each other and support each other.
- Writers choose their form based on their audience and purpose.

DO:
- Write using the "6 Things" format and following co-constructed criteria.
- Show evidence of rereading and revision.

SAY:
- Students will be able to tell what they are writing and for whom they are writing. (audience and purpose)

Grade 2 Free Verse Poetry

Big Ideas: **Bold**

Bullet points: Grade 2 outcomes from Manitoba curriculum

Writers and readers talk and write to share what they know and feel with others:
- make and talk about personal observations
- ask for others' ideas and observations to help discover and explore personal understanding
- express preferences for a variety of oral, literary, and media texts
- develop a sense of self as reader, writer, and illustrator
- connect new information, ideas, and experiences with prior knowledge and experiences
- explain new experiences and understanding
- choose to engage in a variety of shared and independent listening, reading, and viewing experiences using texts from a variety of forms
- generate and contribute ideas on particular topics for oral, written, and visual texts
- share own stories and creations with peers and respond to questions or comments
- connect situations portrayed in oral, literary, and media texts to personal experiences

Writers and readers learn from each other and support each other:
- participate in shared language experiences to celebrate individual and class achievement
- work in a variety of cooperative and collaborative partnership and group structures
- contribute related ideas and information in whole-class and small-group activities
- acknowledge the achievements of others
- rehearse roles and responsibilities in the group process by helping others and asking others for help

Writers can choose to write in different ways or forms depending upon their purpose and audience:
- use a variety of forms to organize and give meaning to familiar experiences, ideas, and information
- create original texts to communicate, and demonstrate understanding of forms and techniques
- recognize that information and ideas can be expressed in a variety of forms and genres
- use a variety of forms for particular audiences and purposes
- demonstrate interest in the sounds of words and word combinations in pattern books, poems, songs, and oral and visual presentations

Writers think about their writing and make it clear and interesting for themselves and their readers:
- arrange ideas and information to make sense
- order ideas to create a beginning, middle, and end in own oral, written, and visual texts
- revise illustrations and representations by adding or deleting words and details to make sense
- form letters and words of consistent size and shape
- print legibly using correct letter formation and spacing
- experiment with words and simple sentence patterns to enhance communication forms
- combine illustrations and written texts to express ideas, feelings, and information
- check work for beginning, middle, and end
- spell familiar words using a variety of strategies
- use periods and question marks as end punctuation

continued on next page

Grade 2 Learning Destination

KNOW:
- One form writers can choose is free verse poetry.
- Free verse poetry does not rhyme, but it still has rhythm and beat.
- Poetry looks different on the page than a story.
- Poems can be about anything.
- The writer decides where lines end.

UNDERSTAND:
- Writers might choose poetry when they want to experiment with words or create pictures, feelings, and different senses for their readers.
- Writers and readers use what they know about sounds, letters, words, and pictures to tell their story for their readers and to keep themselves writing.
- Writers think about their writing and make it clear and interesting for themselves and their readers.
- Writers and readers learn from each other and support each other.

DO:
- Write free verse poetry that meets co-constructed criteria.
- Show evidence of rereading and revision.

SAY:
- Students will be able to tell what they are writing and for whom they are writing.

Grade 5: Fur Trade Unit of Study

Big Ideas in Bold

Bullet Points: Grade 5 Outcomes from Manitoba Curriculum

English Language Arts

Writers enhance and improve their writing for themselves and their readers:
- participate in developing criteria to respond to own and others' oral, written, and visual creations and use the criteria to suggest revisions
- revise for content, organization, and clarity
- write legibly and use appropriate formatting and word processing when composing and revising
- select words, sounds, and images for appropriate connotations, and use varied sentence lengths and structures, including compound sentences
- prepare organized compositions, presentations, reports, and inquiry or research projects using pre-established organizers

Writers follow the rules of writing:
- edit to eliminate fragments and run-on sentences
- know and apply spelling conventions using a variety of strategies (including structural analysis, syllabication, and visual memory) and spelling patterns when editing and proofreading; predict the spelling of unfamiliar words using a variety of resources to confirm correctness
- know how to capitalize and punctuate compound sentences, headings, and titles, and apply these conventions when editing and proofreading

Writers and researchers support and work with others:
- distinguish between on-task and off-task ideas and behaviours in cooperative and collaborative groups, and stay on task; identify and solve group productivity issues
- assume the responsibilities of various group roles; choose roles appropriate for tasks and productivity

continued on next page

- demonstrate sensitivity to appropriate language use when communicating orally
- assess group process using checklists and determine areas for development; set group and individual goals

Writers and researchers think and plan before they begin:
- summarize personal knowledge of a topic in categories to determine information needs
- use personal experiences as a basis for exploring, predicting, and expressing opinions and understanding
- use prior knowledge and experiences selectively to make sense of new information in a variety of contexts
- explain the importance of linking personal perceptions and ideas to new concepts
- formulate general and specific questions to identify information needs
- share personal knowledge of a selected topic to help formulate relevant questions appropriate to a specific audience and purpose for group inquiry or research
- plan topics and goals for historical inquiry and research

Writers and researchers organize ideas for their own and their readers' understanding:
- organize information and ideas into categories (such as who, what, where, when, why, how) using a variety of strategies such as webbing, using graphic organizers, sequencing, charting etc.
- record information in own words, cite authors and titles alphabetically, and provide publication dates of sources
- recognize gaps in the information gathered and locate additional information needed for a particular form, audience, and purpose
- assess knowledge gained through the inquiry or research process, form personal conclusions, and generate new questions for further research or inquiry
- use listening, reading, and viewing experiences as models for organizing ideas in own oral, written, and visual texts
- gather and record information and ideas using a plan

- organize ideas and information in ways that clarify and shape understanding
- appraise ideas for clarity and ask extending questions
- understand and use a variety of forms and genres of oral, literary, and media texts (such as poetry, articles, news reports, documentaries, etc.)
- identify key elements (including plot, setting, and characterization) and techniques (such as colour, music, speed) in oral, literary, and media texts, and explore their impact
- record personal knowledge of a topic and collaborate to generate information for inquiry or research
- answer inquiry or research questions using a variety of information sources (such as newspapers, series by the same writer, scripts, diaries, elders, interviews, trips, oral traditions, etc.)
- determine the usefulness of information for inquiry or research purpose and focus using pre-established criteria
- use a variety of tools (including chapter headings and encyclopedia guide words) to access information and ideas; use visual and auditory cues (such as graphics, voice-overs, scene changes, body language, background music, etc.) to identify key ideas

Social Studies
- select information from oral, visual, material, print, or electronic sources. Examples: maps, atlases, art, songs, artifacts, narratives, legends, biographies, historical fiction
- distinguish between primary and secondary information sources for research
- draw conclusions based on research and evidence
- evaluate personal assumptions based on new information and ideas
- distinguish fact from opinion and interpretation
- assess the validity of information sources. Examples: purpose, context, authenticity, origin, objectivity, evidence, reliability

continued on next page

- interpret information and ideas in a variety of media. Examples: art, music, historical fiction, drama, primary sources
- recognize that interpretations of history are subject to change as new information is uncovered or acknowledged
- draw conclusions based on research and evidence
- evaluate personal assumptions based on new information and ideas
- use language that is respectful of human diversity
- articulate personal beliefs and perspectives on issues
- make decisions that reflect fairness and equality in personal interactions with others
- compare differing accounts of historical events
- support ideas and opinions with information or observations
- present information and ideas orally, visually, concretely, or electronically
- organize and record information in a variety of formats, and reference sources appropriately. Examples: maps, charts, outlines, concept maps
- collaborate with others to establish and carry out group goals and responsibilities
- use a variety of strategies to resolve conflicts peacefully and fairly. Examples: clarification, negotiation, compromise
- make decisions that reflect fairness and equality in personal interactions with others
- negotiate constructively with others to build consensus and solve problems
- recognize bias and discrimination and propose solutions

Grade 5 Learning Destination

Big Ideas from ELA and Social Studies Curricula related to the researching and writing:
- Social scientists think and plan before they begin their research.
- Social scientists enhance and improve their writing for themselves and their readers.
- Social scientists follow the conventions of writing to make their writing more understandable and interesting for their readers.
- Social scientists support and work with others.
- Social scientists organize their ideas for their own and their readers' understanding.

KNOW:
- The conventions of non-fiction report writing.

UNDERSTAND:
- The purpose of this genre is to communicate learning with others.
- Making writing interesting in expository writing is done differently than in narrative writing.

DO:
- Think and plan before beginning research.
- Research and write on a topic from the fur trade following co-constructed criteria.
- Write about one or more topics for a class book about the fur trade.
- Work collaboratively with a partner on one section of the book.

SAY:
- Be able to articulate the purpose and audience for this inquiry.

Appendix B: Assessment Plans

- Grade 2: 6 Things You Should Know About My Community
- Grade 1/2 Free Verse Poetry

Grade 2: 6 Things You Should Know About My Community*
Learning Destination

KNOW:
- One form writers can write in is a "6 Things" format.
- Sometimes writers write to teach their readers and to show what they know.

UNDERSTAND:
- Writers and readers use what they know about sounds, letters, words, and pictures to tell their story for their readers and to keep themselves writing.
- Writers think about their writing and make it clear and interesting for themselves and their readers.
- Writers and readers learn from each other and support each other.

DO:
- Write in the 6 Things format following the co-constructed criteria.
- Show evidence of rereading and revision.

SAY:
- Students will be able to tell what they are writing and for whom they are writing.

Descriptions of Quality (Models/Samples/Frontloading)

- Criteria for writing 6 Things
- One or two teacher models
- Practice using the criteria
- One to three shared writes
- Scaffolded conversations before students start to write
- Descriptive feedback

*Adapted from ESPN magazine

Evidence We Could Collect

CONVERSATIONS
- Listen in during turn and talk
- One-to-one conferences: Ask students whom they are writing for and why.
- Pause and think: Sit in circle and respond to one of two prompts (one thing I am going to do when I start writing or one question I have about writing in the "6 Things You Should Know About" format).
- All Talk: Discuss one thing they are going to do when they start writing; and one way they met the criteria today.
- Aurasma (an app that can be used to link a video of a student talking with a paper copy of the work)

OBSERVATIONS
- Focus Questions on anecdotal record sheets: Is the student demonstrating active listening? Is the student staying on topic during turn and talk? Is the student using the language the teacher is planting? Can the student keep on writing? Is the student rereading?

PRODUCTS
- Look at writing samples.
- Check the writing for evidence of key criteria: Is there evidence of cross-outs and changing ideas? Is the student sourcing the room? Is the student using the format?
- Consider exit slips.
- Explain Everything App (an app that can be used to record student writing as it is happening and the audio of their thinking)

Evaluation (What defines meeting expectations?)

The writer:
- meets criteria.
- shows evidence of rereading and revising in draft copy.
- articulates audience and purpose of this writing project.
- writes independently when responsibility is released.
- shows evidence of thinking about the reader.
- displays evidence of editing for ending punctuation, capitals at the start of sentences, and correct spelling of word wall words in published copy.

Grade 1/2 Free Verse Poetry

Learning Destination

KNOW:
- One form writers can write is free verse poetry. Free verse poetry does not rhyme.
- Poetry looks different on the page than a story.
- Poems can be about anything.

UNDERSTAND:
- Writers and readers use what they know about sounds, letters, words, and pictures to tell their story for their readers and to keep themselves writing.
- Writers think about their writing and make it clear and interesting for themselves and their readers.
- Writers and readers learn from each other and support each other.

DO:
- Write free verse poetry that meets co-constructed criteria.
- Show evidence of rereading and revision.

SAY:
- Students will be able to tell what they are writing and for whom they are writing. They will describe the audience and purpose.

Descriptions of Quality (Models/Samples/Frontloading)

- Criteria for writing free verse poetry
- One or two teacher models
- Practice using the criteria
- One to three shared writes
- Scaffolded conversations before students start to write
- Celebrations (Descriptive feedback)

Evidence We Could Collect

CONVERSATIONS
- Listen in during turn and talk.
- One-to-one conferences: Ask students whom they are writing for and why.
- Pause and think: Sit in circle and respond to one of two prompts (one thing they are going to do when they start writing their poem or one question they have about writing free verse poetry.
- All Talk: Discuss one thing they are going to do when they start writing their poem.
- Aurasma (an app that can be used to link a video of a student talking with a paper copy of the work)

OBSERVATIONS
- Focus Questions on anecdotal record sheets: Is the student demonstrating active listening? Is the student staying on topic during turn and talk? Is the student using the language the teacher is planting? Can the student keep on writing? Is the student rereading?

PRODUCTS
- Look at the writing samples.
- Check the writing for evidence of key criteria: Does it look like a poem? Is there evidence of cross-outs and changing ideas? Is the student sourcing the room?

Evaluation (What defines fully meeting expectations?)

The writer:
- meets criteria.
- shows evidence of rereading and revising in draft copy.
- articulates audience and purpose of this writing project.
- writes independently when responsibility is released.
- shows evidence of thinking about the reader.
- displays evidence of editing for ending punctuation, capitals at the start of sentences, and correct spelling of word wall words in published copy.

Bibliography

Calkins, L. 2010. *Launch an Intermediate Writing Workshop: Getting Started with Units of Study for Teaching Writing, Grades 3-5*. Portsmouth, NH: Heinemann.

Campbell Hill, B. 2001. *Developmental Continuums: A Framework for Literary Instruction and Assessment K-8*. Norwood, MA: Christopher-Gordon Publishers.

Collins, K. 2004. *Growing Readers: Units of Study in the Primary Classroom*. Portland, ME: Stenhouse Publishers.

Crooks, T. 1988. The impact of classroom evaluation practices on students. *Review of Educational Research* Vol. 58(4): 438-481.

Davies, A. 2000. *Making Classroom Assessment Work*, 1st Edition. Courtenay, BC: Connections Publishing.

Davies, A. 2011. *Making Classroom Assessment Work*, 3rd Edition. Courtenay, BC: Connections Publishing.

Dweck, C. 2006. *Mindset: The New Psychology of Success*. New York: Ballantine Books.

Gallagher, K. 2006. *Teaching Adolescent Writers*. Portland, ME: Stenhouse Publishers.

Graves, D. H. 2003. *Writing: Teachers and Children at Work*. Portsmouth, NH: Heinemann.

Gregory, K., Cameron, C., & Davies, A. 2011a. *Setting and Using Criteria*, 2nd Edition. Courtenay, BC: Connections Publishing.

Gregory, K., Cameron, C., & Davies, A. 2011b. *Self-Assessment and Goal Setting*, 2nd Edition. Courtenay, BC: Connections Publishing.

Hattie, J. 2011. *Visible Learning for Teachers: Maximizing Impact on Learning.* London, UK: Routledge.

Johnston, P. 2012. *Opening Minds: Using Language to Change Lives.* Portland, ME: Stenhouse Publishers.

Kittle, P. 2008. *Write Beside Them: Risk, Voice, and Clarity in High School Writing.* Portsmouth, NH: Heinemann.

Lincoln, Y., & Guba, E. 1984. *Naturalistic Inquiry.* Beverly Hills, CA: SAGE.

Maxwell, G.S., & Cumming, J.J. 2011. Managing without public examinations: Successful and sustained curriculum and assessment reform in Queensland. In L. Yates, C. Collins, & K. O'Connor (Eds.), *Australia's Curriculum Dilemmas: State Perspectives and Changing Times* (pp. 202-222). Melbourne, AU: Melbourne University Press.

Miller, D. 2012. *Reading with Meaning: Teaching Comprehension in the Primary Grades*, 2nd Edition. Portland, ME: Stenhouse Publishers.

Natriello, G. 1987. The impact of evaluation processes on students. *Educational Psychologist* Vol. 22(2): 155-175.

Pearson, P.D., & Gallagher, M. 1983. The instruction of reading apprehension. *Contemporary Educational Psychology* Vol. 8(3): 317-344.

Routman, R. 2005. *Writing Essentials: Raising Expectations and Results While Simplifying Teaching.* Portsmouth, NH: Heinemann.

Stiggins, R. 2004. *Student-Involved Assessment FOR Learning*, 4th Edition. Upper Saddle River, NJ: Pearson Prentice Hall.

Stiggins, R. 2014. *Revolutionize Assessment: Empower Students, Inspire Learning.* Newbury Park, CA: Corwin.

Stiggins, R., & Bridgeford, N. 1985. The ecology of classroom assessment. *Journal of Educational Measurement.* Vol. 22(4): 271-286.

Tomlinson, C.A., & Moon, T. 2013. *Assessment and Student Success in a Differentiated Classroom.* Alexandria, VA: ASCD.

Wiggins, G., & McTighe, J. 2005. *Understanding by Design*, 2nd Edition. Alexandria, VA: ASCD.

Brenda Augusta is a teacher, consultant, mentor, presenter, and author. She acquired her deep understanding of assessment, literacy, and numeracy in her years as a curriculum consultant for a large urban school division. Her passion for supporting educators in ways that honour, encourage, and inspire began here and continues to grow as she facilitates professional learning with schools, districts, and organizations across Canada. Brenda uses her ongoing classroom-based work as a way to ensure that her writing and presenting offer practical, engaging, and research-validated ideas that foster a positive impact on student learning. She has co-authored two other books — *design/ed*, design ideas for educators and learning environments, and *Lesson Study: Powerful Assessment and Professional Practice*, a book for leaders describing how to use the principles of assessment in the service of learning with adult learners involved in school-based professional development.

Resources from connect2learning

The following books and multimedia resources are available from connect2learning. Discounts are available on bulk orders.

Classroom Assessment Resources

La collecte de preuves et les portfolios : la participation des élèves
  à la documentation pédagogique.................................. ISBN 978-1-928092-09-4
Making Physical Education Instruction and Assessment Work .... ISBN 978-1-928092-08-7
Collecting Evidence and Portfolios: Engaging Students in Pedagogical
  Documentation .... ISBN 978-1-928092-05-6
Grading, Reporting, and Professional Judgment in Elementary Classrooms .. ISBN 978-1-928092-03-2
Making Writing Instruction Work .... ISBN 978-1-928092-02-5
Making Classroom Assessment Work – Third Edition .... ISBN 978-0-9867851-2-2
L'évaluation en cours d'apprentissage .... ISBN 978-2-7650-1800-1
Quality Assessment in High Schools: Accounts From Teachers .... ISBN 978-0-9867851-5-3
A Fresh Look at Grading and Reporting in High Schools .... ISBN 978-0-9867851-6-0
Setting and Using Criteria – Second Edition .... ISBN 978-0-9783193-9-7
Établir et utiliser des critères – Deuxième édition .... ISBN 978-0-9867851-7-7
Self-Assessment and Goal Setting – Second Edition .... ISBN 978-0-9867851-0-8
L'autoévaluation et la détermination des objectifs - Deuxième édition .... ISBN 978-0-9867851-9-1
Conferencing and Reporting – Second Edition .... ISBN 978-0-9867851-1-5
Rencontres et communication de l'apprentissage - Deuxième édition .... ISBN 978-1-928092-00-1

Leaders' and Facilitators' Resources

Residency: Powerful Assessment and Professional Practice .... ISBN 978-0-928092-04-9
Lesson Study: Powerful Assessment and Professional Practice .... ISBN 978-0-9867851-8-4
Leading the Way to Assessment for Learning: A Practical Guide .... ISBN 978-0-9867851-3-9
Transforming Schools and Systems Using Assessment:
  A Practical Guide .... ISBN 978-0-9867851-4-6
Protocols for Professional Learning Conversations .... ISBN 978-0-9682160-7-1
When Students Fail to Learn .... ISBN 978-0-9783193-7-3
Assessment for Learning K-12 (Multimedia) .... ISBN 978-0-9783193-8-0
Assessment of Learning: Standards-Based Grading and Reporting
  (Multimedia) .... ISBN 978-0-9736352-8-7
Facilitator's Guide to Classroom Assessment K-12 (Multimedia) .... ISBN 978-0-9736352-0-1

How To Order

Phone: (800) 603-9888 (toll-free North America)
        (250) 703-2920
Fax: (250) 703-2921

Web: connect2learning.com
Post: connect2learning
        2449D Rosewall Crescent
        Courtenay, BC, V9N 8R9
        Canada

E-mail: books@connect2learning.com

connect2learning also sponsors events, workshops, and web conferences on assessment and other education-related topics, both for classroom teachers and school and district leaders. Please contact us for a full catalogue.